HOLIDAYS, HOLY DAYS, AND OTHER BIG DAYS FOR YOUTH

HOLIDAYS, HOLY DAYS, AND OTHER BIG DAYS FOR YOUTH
100 IDEAS FOR YOUTH MINISTRY

Scripture quotations in this publication are from the Contemporary English Version Bible. Copyright © American Bible Society, 1995. Used by permission.

To Ty,
who has been like a brother to me

99 00 01 02 03 04 05 06 07 08—10 9 8 7 6 5 4 3 2 1

MANUFACTURED IN THE UNITED STATES OF AMERICA

HOLIDAYS, HOLY DAYS, AND OTHER BIG DAYS FOR YOUTH

Ideas for Youth Ministry

Todd Outcalt

Abingdon Press
Nashville

ACKNOWLEDGMENTS

Many thanks to my friends at Abingdon Press who have worked hard to make this book a reality. I am especially indebted to Eric Skinner for his dedication and helpfulness.

I also thank the many colleagues who have given time and talent to teenagers. I've enjoyed working with you and cherish your friendship. Heartfelt thanks to Joe Mitchell, Frank VanAllen, Tom Heaton, Larry and Rita Gardner, Doug Hales, Jeff Buck, Roger Gardner, Tom Blackford, and Meg Lassiat—among a long list of folks who have taught me much.

As always, love to Becky, Chelsey, and Logan for offering up the time and space for me to write this book.

CONTENTS

YOUTH MINISTRY DURING HOLIDAYS, HOLY DAYS, AND OTHER TIMES

Teenagers are natural born party animals. If there is a celebration going on, a holiday to observe, you can bet they will catch the spirit of the day—even if the moment has something to do with faith, and God, and remembering a bit of history.

I recall that when I was a teenager, I went to youth meetings each week in the shadow of a giant wall plaque bearing the words of the Ten Commandments (in King James English no less). There the words of the fourth commandment stared down at me with a relentless heaviness: "Remember the Sabbath day, to keep it holy." Then, those words seemed shot through with a quaint nostalgia, as I regarded their mystery by coming to church each Sunday, sitting in the customary pew with my family, seeing familiar faces in church week after week, singing the same hymns. But the word *holy* seemed distant to me, as if the very word itself contained some type of magic or grace that I could neither experience nor explain.

To make something "holy," of course—whether a day, an object, or a place—is to set it apart, to regard the thing itself as belonging to the domain of God. Jewish faith and tradition, it seems to me, retains a much stronger sense of this original meaning than the Christian counterpart. For, although most Christians regard certain days and places as having a sense of "otherness," Protestant tradition has little in the way of holy things, holy days (other than Christmas and Easter, of course), and minor holidays that are celebrated with any passion or unity of purpose.

Nevertheless, holy days and holidays abound, both as part and parcel of the church year and within the broader spectrum of national observances. Furthermore, there are days in the lives of teenagers that take on mystical proportions—graduation, birthdays, obtaining a driver's license, just to name a few. Wise youth leaders do well to make the most of these special days, as they often provide doorways into the hearts of our kids.

This book, then, is not simply about those "holy" days that we observe within the church but also about those holidays and special occasions that roll around each year. What teenager, for example, would refuse a celebration of Valentine's Day, or April Fool's Day, or even souped up versions of Pentecost or the Fourth of July? All of these days and more are opportunities for us to enter the lives of our youth in meaningful ways. Some of the days may not be "holy," or even "holi-days," but they are certainly special in the eyes of many teenagers.

Most of all, I hope that this book will provide helpful ideas for ministry with teenagers and their families. Youth have always had much to offer the church, our communities, and our world. If we can help youth bridge the gap from the mundane to the holy through these special days, their faith will grow into something beautiful and deep.

HOW TO USE THIS BOOK

Toward that end I have included a host of learning opportunities and fun, which can be used to celebrate most of the major, minor, and in some cases, very minor days of the church year and calendar. Leaders will also find a mixture of ideas that can be used as lessons, friendship-building moments, affirmations, worship, drama, service, training and counseling sessions, and games. In many instances, I have included more than one idea for a particular day as well as themes that can be used to guide the selection of a particular event.

A casual glance through the book will reveal several observations. First, the book is organized according to the church year and not the yearly calendar. Hence, I have chosen to begin with the Advent season (winter) and move through the seasons toward Easter (spring), the long days of Pentecost (summer), and the approach of Thanksgiving (fall). Each theme bears the name of the holiday or special day being observed.

I have also intentionally included activities that push the boundaries of thought as well as those activities that require little preparation. My hope is that you might be able to find both lessons and leadership sessions that can be used with more spiritually adept teenagers, as well as lighter fare for those teenagers who may be new to the faith or who are still searching.

In addition, I have included several special days in the summer section of this book. Here you can find several activities that can be used at church camps, during summer vacation and driver's education, and a host of birthday ideas.

Finally, there are many ways to use the topics and lessons in this book. You are limited only by your own creativity and vision. You may wish to think of this book as a guide to the special days of the year, but you can provide the focus and spiritual approach for your teens.

Toward that end, I hope that you experience many holidays, holy days, and other special times with your youth. The memories of these days may be enough to last a lifetime.

Holidays, Holy Days, and Other Big Days for Youth is the third volume of a trilogy designed to be a comprehensive resource of youth ministry ideas. The first book in the series, *Seeing is Believing!*, contains one hundred object talks for a variety of themes and situations. The second book, *The Heat is On!*, is loaded with summertime ideas for mission trips, retreats, and other special youth gatherings. This volume, *Holidays, Holy Days, and Other Big Days for Youth*, will provide dozens of wonderful ideas for special events throughout the year. I hope that this trilogy will be a useful resource for all who work with teenagers and who seek to share their faith.

CHAPTER ONE: WINTER

#1: GOD SQUAD

Themes: ADVENT, CONCERN FOR OTHERS

Scripture: I will answer your prayers
because I have set a time when I will help by coming
to save you (Isaiah 49:8).

Preparation: a sack of small rocks

The Worship, The Prayer

Close your youth meeting with this worship time. Say:

Did you know that in the Jewish faith, people place rocks on tombstones instead of flowers? This tradition probably dates back to the time when people used to mark graves with stones, which were more permanent and abiding than plants, such as flowers or trees. In our worship today, let's each take a stone as a way of remembering someone who needs our prayers.

After each teenager has taken a rock, have the group form a circle. Then read aloud the Scripture. Ask the youth to think of someone in the youth group, in their family, or among their friends who needs a prayer. Have silent prayer or offer spoken prayers for these individuals. Sing a song together.

Then say:

After we leave today, I would like for you to place your stone in a location that is meaningful to you—in your room, in your school locker, in your car—and it will remind you to pray for others this week.

#2: SOMETHING OLD, SOMETHING NEW

Themes: ADVENT, PREPARING FOR CHRIST'S BIRTH

Scripture: "Clear a path in the desert! Make a straight road for the LORD our God" (Isaiah 40:3).

Preparation: a broken toy (or a stuffed animal that has lost its stuffing), duct tape, paper clips, and glue

The Lesson

Begin the lesson by asking your group to fix the broken toy so that it would be presentable to a child. If you have a larger group, you may need more than one broken toy. Give your group five to seven minutes to complete the task.

Then ask:

Why was it difficult to fix the toy? Why was it difficult to take something old and make it look like new? Allow a few minutes for discussion. Read aloud the Scripture above (or a longer version of Isaiah 40).

Then say:

The prophet Isaiah lived during a time when there were great social upheavals. Foreign armies were threatening to invade Israel; and after Jerusalem was captured, many people were taken away into captivity in a distant land. It appeared that there was no hope for the future. But Isaiah refused to believe that God would abandon the people. He envisioned a time when all the crooked ways would be made straight and all of that was broken would be made right again.

Advent is the time when we prepare for Christ's arrival. To do this, we need to prepare ourselves spiritually, thinking about God's ways and what God would have us be. We can also try to envision the ways that God might call us to set our world right again.

Then ask:

What are some of the evidences of a broken world that you see around you? What might God be asking us to do? How might we respond to God's call?

#3: FEAR NOT!

Themes: ADVENT, PREPARING FOR JESUS

Scripture: Then the angel told Mary, "Don't be afraid! God is pleased with you, and you will have a son. His name will be Jesus" (Luke 1:30-31).

Preparation: index cards and pencils

The Lesson

Give each teen an index card and pencil. Then ask the teenagers to write a top ten list of the things that frighten them most. After they have completed their list, divide them into small groups or ask each teen to read aloud his or her list.

Then say:

One of the most frequent phrases in the Bible are "Do not be afraid!" The angel tells Mary, "Don't be afraid." And later, Jesus told his disciples over and over, "Do not be afraid." As our lists indicate, you and I have many fears in life. We are afraid of making mistakes, afraid of dying, afraid of spiders, afraid of certain diseases and maybe certain people. But Advent can be a time of hearing the good news of God's presence.

In Hebrew, the name *Jesus* means "The Lord (Yahweh) is salvation." Advent is a time of remembering that we can anticipate our salvation in Jesus, that we can be set free of our fears, that we need not be afraid of tomorrow—no matter what happens.

Ask the youth to talk in small groups about ways they have experienced God's salvation and protection. Close by discussing the question "Can you think of ways we can demonstrate our trust in God's help and salvation?"

#4: TAKIN' IT TO THE STREETS

Themes: ADVENT, HOPE

Scripture: The LORD God has told us what is right. . . .
"See that justice is done,
let mercy be your first concern,
and humbly obey your God" (Micah 6:8).

Preparation: pocket crosses, card stock and markers, instruments and hymnals or Christmas songbooks

The Service Project

During the Advent/Christmas season, many people become more giving and concerned for the poor. Use the Advent season to its best advantage by challenging your group with one of the service projects listed below:

1. Purchase inexpensive pocket crosses and take to the streets to give the crosses away to shoppers and other busy people. Give everyone a kind word along with your gift and/or a printed invitation to attend an Advent/Christmas service at your church. Ask your pastor for a list of the times and dates of the services.

2. Have the youth use card stock to create bookmarks or Christmas cards with Bible verses or hopeful messages written on them. Have the youth decorate the bookmarks or cards and take them to a local food panty, shelter, mission, or residential care center.

3. Ask a store manager if your group can provide Christmas music near a Salvation Army kettle. Most stores that allow Salvation Army ringers will allow your group to sing or play selections of Christmas music for people as they pass in and out of the doors.

Winter
#5: LIGHTS OUT!

Themes: ADVENT, PREPARING FOR CHRIST

Scripture: Stand up! Shine! Your new day is dawning (Isaiah 60:1).

Preparation: a candle (with stand) or an oil lamp filled with oil, matches

The Lesson

This lesson works best at night, or in a room where sunlight cannot filter in. Begin by gathering the youth into a circle around the candle (or lamp) while the lights are on. Ask each teen to discuss the following question with a partner: What, do you think, is the most important ingredient for human life and for life on earth?

After brief discussion, ask teens to offer their insights. Then say:

During the Advent season, we in the northern hemisphere notice that the days get shorter. There is less sunlight and more darkness. December 21 is the day of least sunlight. After this time, the days begin to slowly lengthen again. When we think about the importance of light in our world, we know that it is one of the most crucial elements for life. Without light, in fact, there could be no life as we know it—no warmth, no food, nothing. Long ago, the prophets spoke of light as a metaphor for God. They spoke of God's reign and the light that would appear to all people. Likewise, you and I can walk in darkness; or we can choose to follow the light of God.

Turn out the lights and sit together in darkness and silence for awhile.

Then ask:

What thoughts come to mind as you sit in darkness? Are you comfortable or uncomfortable? Why?

Light the candle. Then ask:

How does the presence of light make you feel? Why, do you think, did the prophets speak of light as a metaphor for God?

Close by singing Advent/Christmas songs around the candle.

#6: BACK TO THE FUTURE

Themes: CHRISTMAS, BIRTH OF JESUS, DISCIPLESHIP

Scripture: [Mary] gave birth to her first-born son. She dressed him in baby clothes and laid him on a bed of hay, because there was no room for them in the inn (Luke 2:7).

Preparation: first-century costumes or other attire for a reenactment of Jesus' birth, Bibles

The Drama

The story of Jesus' birth is a wonderful opportunity to engage the youth in drama. Divide your group into two teams. Give each group costumes, a Bible, and these instructions: I'd like each group to prepare a three- to five-minute skit based on the story of Jesus' birth. One group will prepare a skit based on Luke 2:1-7. The other group will prepare a skit based on Luke 2:8-21.

Give each group twenty to thirty minutes to prepare and to costume the actors. After each group has acted out their skit, gather the group together for these questions:

• What was most difficult about this assignment?

• What emotions did you attempt to convey?

• What does the story of Jesus' birth teach us about life? hope? faith?

#7: TWELVE DAYS OF CHRISTMAS

Themes: CHRISTMAS, CELEBRATION

Scripture: As the shepherds returned to their sheep, they were praising God and saying wonderful things about him (Luke 2:20).

Preparation: photocopies of the list below

Friendship-Building

Have you ever wanted a quick and easy ministry idea for those twelve days between Christmas and Epiphany? As a song says, there are twelve days of Christmas; and here's a new way for youth to keep in touch with one another during the holiday season. At your last youth meeting prior to Christmas, photocopy the list below for each teenager. Encourage and challenge the youth to follow the instructions for each day of Christmas.

1st Day of Christmas (Christmas Day): Call up a friend in the group and say, "Merry Christmas. Jesus loves you!"

2nd Day: Read Matthew 1:18-25 before you go to bed.

3rd Day: Write a letter to a family member who lives far away.

4th Day: Make a top ten list of things you are thankful for.

5th Day: Call up a friend and invite him/her to our next youth meeting.

6th Day: Send a postcard of thanks to your pastor, a volunteer youth leader, or someone who has helped you recently.

7th Day: Do something nice (and unexpected) for your mom or dad.

8th Day: Get together with at least two friends from the youth group for one hour.

9th Day: Read two Psalms before you go to bed.

10th Day: Do something outside with a friend from the youth group.

11th Day: Read the first chapter of a good book.

12th Day: Read Matthew 2:1-12 before you go to bed.

#8: AFTER-CHRISTMAS BLUES

Themes: CHRISTMAS, DEPRESSION, LONELINESS

Scripture: Praise God in heaven!
Peace on earth to everyone who pleases God! (Luke 2:14).

Preparation: a list of Scripture references (see below)

Peer Counseling

Many people experience bouts of depression and loneliness before or after Christmas. Some teenagers in your youth group may also experience these feelings, particularly if they see only one parent at Christmas, if their friends are vacationing, if they have experienced a recent death in the family, or if they have had difficulties in school. Use the Christmas break to offer some peer counseling to teens who may be feeling blue.

Identify the more mature and spiritually deep teenagers in your group. Ask these teens if they would be willing to make themselves available for other teens who may want to talk by phone over the holiday season. Get these volunteers together for a brief training session before Christmas and provide them with helpful suggestions for talking to peers and offering positive words.

Give each peer counselor a list of these Scripture references (and add others of your own if you would like):

Depression: Psalm 30; Isaiah 35

Discouragement: Habakkuk 1:1-3; 1 John 5:1-15

Drug and Alcohol Problems: Romans 7:14-25; 1 Corinthians 6:12-20

Loneliness: Psalm 68:1-10; Psalm 137:1-6

Then list in your newsletter or December mailing the names of the peer counselors and their phone numbers. Keep in touch with the counselors in case they need your help.

#9: CHRISTMAS CANDY

Themes: CHRISTMAS, MATERIALISM

Scripture: Every good and perfect gift comes down from the Father (James 1:17).

Preparation: Christmas chocolates or other small candies, whiteboard and marker (optional)

Discussion Starter

Give each teenager a piece of candy and ask him or her to eat it. Then ask:

What is it that makes candy so appealing? (Write answers on a whiteboard if you would like).

Then say:

Like candy, the things we desire in life can be appealing for awhile; but then we want something more. No matter how many things we get at Christmas, we will eventually wear them out or we will forget about them in a few months or years. Things never satisfy us. What we desire comes from God. Many years ago, St. Augustine wrote: "We are restless until we find our rest in God."

Gather everyone into a circle (or into smaller groups if you would like). Read aloud the Scripture passage and then ask the youth to discuss the following questions:

- What are the gifts that God gives?

- What is lasting about these gifts?

- Why do we need them?

- Do you think that these gifts will satisfy us?

#10: CHRISTMAS EVE

Themes: CHRISTMAS, JOY

Scripture: I am creating new heavens and a new earth; everything of the past will be forgotten (Isaiah 65:17).

Preparation: helium-filled balloons, string

The Worship

Before this worship time, prepare the helium balloons and tie a string onto each one (you could also purchase these quite easily). When the teens gather for worship, begin by singing a Christmas hymn, such as "Joy to the World" or "Hark the Herald Angels Sing." Ask the youth to offer prayers of thanksgiving or other thoughts on what Christmas means to them. Give each teen a balloon, and invite one of the youth to read aloud the Scripture lesson.

Say:

One of the most dominating images in the Bible is the notion that God is always doing something new. The psalmist wrote, "Sing a new song" (Psalm 33:3). Isaiah said that God said, "I am creating something new" (Isaiah 43:19). And again, we read that God is preparing a new heaven and a new earth. Christmas Eve is a wonderful time to renew our faith, to stretch toward God's future and the promises that God has offered in Jesus. Like the balloon that you hold in your hand, God is always pulling us toward a new future, toward new horizons and hopes. We can't remain where we are forever. We have to be willing to grow.

Ask the youth to work in pairs or small groups to offer words of encouragement to one another. Invite them to discuss the following questions:

- What new thing is God doing in my life?

- Where is God leading me?

Close your worship time with prayer and the singing of another Christmas hymn, such as "Silent Night" or "Away in a Manger."

#11: THE GIFT

Themes: CHRISTMAS, MYSTERY

Scripture: Jesus Christ never changes! He is the same yesterday, today, and forever (Hebrews 13:8).

Preparation: a beautifully wrapped box with a picture of Jesus inside

The Crowdbreaker

Begin the youth meeting with this crowdbreaker. Gather everyone into a circle and allow each teenager to shake or feel the package as it is passed around the group.

Then ask:

What do you think is inside the box? (Allow responses.) Which would you prefer—to look at the beautiful wrapping on the box or to look inside the box?

Say:

When we stop to think about it, life is filled with many mysteries and discoveries. In the church, we call the sacraments (baptism and the Lord's Supper) "holy mysteries." The apostle Paul talked about the mystery of the Resurrection (1 Corinthians 15:51). We yearn to look inside God's mercy—like this beautiful package—and discover what is there. Likewise, we yearn to discover for ourselves the greatest of God's gifts: the gift of Jesus. Being a follower of Jesus is not about believing certain propositions or ideas; we become disciples when we have discovered Jesus for ourselves and we have learned to follow him.

Open the box and pass it around the circle, allowing the youth to look inside.

Say:

Christmas is a time to remind ourselves that Jesus is our gift. He is the one who makes all other gifts possible.

#12: JINGLE ALL THE WAY

Themes: CHRISTMAS

Scripture: Let all things praise the name of the LORD (Psalm 148:5).

Preparation: a sleigh bell or other small noisemaker, two blindfolds

The Game

After forming a large circle with your entire group, choose two teenagers to begin the game. Blindfold both persons, place them in the center of the circle, and give one of the teens a bell.

Then say:

The object of this game is twofold: The person with the bell will attempt to flee from the person without the bell, and the person without the bell must attempt to tag the person who has the bell. The person holding the bell cannot speak but must ring the bell every time the other person says, "Jingle."

To begin play, both persons will begin maneuvering inside the circle. Each time the person without the bell says, "Jingle," the person with the bell must give the bell a shake. Those teens forming the circle will serve as the boundary and will also help keep both players from running into each other (be sure to keep the circle large).

After one minute, call time. If the player without the bell has not tagged the player with the bell, a new player without a bell is blindfolded. Continue play until everyone has had an opportunity to participate. This is a fun game and is quite funny to watch.

#13: TO THE WORLD, WITH LOVE

Themes: EPIPHANY, GOD'S LOVE, THE CHURCH

Scripture: From the beginning you were told that we must love each other (1 John 3:11).

Preparation: a copy of the form letter, below, for each teenager

Discussion Starter/Lesson

Give each teen a copy of the form letter below (or retype it in larger format).

Say:

Epiphany is a celebration of God's revelation to all people of the earth. In Jesus, God sent a love letter to the world. If God were to send an actual letter today, however, what would it say? Take a few moments to write a letter for God to the world.

After the youth have completed their letters, allow each teen to read his or hers or have the teens discuss their letters in small groups.

To the World:

Today I hope that you will remember

The most important thing I want to say to you is

Please try to get along. I am here to help you with

The best things I have given you are

Yours always and forever,

The Almighty

#14: Beggars and Kings

Themes: EPIPHANY, INCLUSIVENESS

Scripture: Faith in Christ Jesus is what makes each of you equal with each other, whether you are a Jew or a Greek, a slave or a free person, a man or a woman (Galatians 3:28).

Preparation: newspapers, scissors, Bibles

The Lesson

Divide the group into teams of three or four. Give team group a small stack of newspapers. Read aloud and reflect as a group upon the Scripture passage.

Say:

I'd like for you to look through the newspapers and cut out stories or photographs that demonstrate how people can work together in spite of their differences. Once you have a couple of examples, prepare to explain to the rest of the group what you found.

Give adequate time for each team to complete the task and then invite each team to talk about their findings. Then give each group one of the following Scripture passages: John 15:5-8; John 17:20-23; Philippians 1:27-28. Ask each team to read and reflect upon their passage.

Then ask:

What type of unity is being talked about in your Scripture passage? How are the barriers that separate people being broken down? Based upon your passage, what do you think God desires of us?

Follow this discussion by asking individuals to give examples of ways they have seen the barriers of racism and sexism being broken down in our world and in the church. Close with prayers for the church, then once again read aloud the Scripture passage from Galatians.

#15: YOU LIGHT UP MY LIFE

Themes: EPIPHANY, HOPE

Scripture: My friends, what good is it to say you have faith, when you don't do anything to show that you really do have faith? (James 2:14).

Preparation: small flashlights (with batteries), boxes of Lego® building blocks, a picture of the ancient Temple in Jerusalem

Friendship-Building

Epiphany has long been symbolized by images of light. This friendship-building exercise works best at night or in a dark room.

Begin by dividing the group into teams of three or four. Give each team a small flashlight, a box of Legos®, and a picture of the temple.

Then say:

In a moment I am going to turn out the lights. Each team must work together to build a replica of the ancient Temple. You will have ten minutes, and you must work together using only the flashlight and Legos® provided.

After ten minutes, turn on the lights and see which team has done the best job or has built the best replica. Ask each team to respond to the following questions:

• What made this task difficult or easy?

• How did you learn to work together?

#16: NEW BEGINNING

Themes: NEW YEAR'S EVE, RENEWAL, FORGIVENESS

Scripture: Everything on earth has its own time and its own season (Ecclesiastes 3:1).

Preparation: a large calendar from the past year, paper, pencils, Bibles

The Lesson

Tear off the individual sheets of the calendar (one for each month) and fasten them to the wall. Hand out the paper and pencils.

Say:

Every new year presents an opportunity for us to make a new start. A new year also gives us an opportunity to look back over a year passed and to see how far we have come. Use your paper and pencils to write about something significant that happened to you in each month of this past year. Think about events in your life that were joyous or traumatic, that were accomplishments or struggles.

Afterward, divide the group into pairs and ask each person to talk about his or her list of important events. Then read John 3:16-21 aloud.

Say:

As you consider what you did in the past year, were there times when you needed God's forgiveness? How did God help you through the tough times?

Close by inviting the youth to write down the important events that took place in the youth group during the past year. They can record these on the calendar pages attached to the wall.

Ask:

What important events do you hope we can repeat this year? What resolutions do you think our group needs to make together?

Invite someone to read aloud Ecclesiastes 3:1-8 as a closing prayer.

#17: OUT WITH THE OLD, IN WITH THE NEW

Themes: NEW YEAR, FUN

Scripture: We make our own plans,
but the LORD decides where we will go (Proverbs 16:9).

Preparation: paper and pencils, markerboard or large sheets of paper, markers

The Game

This is a fun New Year's game that can be played much like Pictionary® or Charades.

First, divide the group into two teams (boys against girls always creates excitement). Hand out paper and pencils, and ask each team to write down phrases or titles of key events from the past year. This could include movies, television shows, important news items, celebrities, and so forth.

To play, a person from each team will draw a slip of paper from the other team and, without talking, will have two minutes to draw or act out what is on the paper. Keep score if you like. Make sure that each team has an equal number of chances and that everyone on each team takes a turn drawing or acting out.

#18: BEGIN AGAIN

Themes: NEW YEAR, FRIENDSHIP, DISCIPLESHIP

Scripture: At that time the people will turn and trust their Creator, the holy God of Israel (Isaiah 17:7).

Preparation: paper and pencils, a diploma, Bibles

The Devotion

After handing out the paper and pencils, ask someone to read aloud Proverbs 8 (or students may take turns reading verses).

Then say:

The Book of Proverbs is often called a book of wisdom, because it contains many wise sayings. As you have heard in this passage, wisdom is the beginning of a happy life. Honesty and sound judgment are also important. We need wisdom to make sound decisions in life. At the beginning of a new year, many people make resolutions. These resolutions are like promises that we make to ourselves, promises that can help us live a better life.

Hold up the diploma. Say:

Even though we cannot earn a diploma in wisdom, we can learn to be wise by living a life of justice, mercy and forgiveness. Perhaps the most important promises we can make to ourselves involve our attitudes, our spiritual growth, and our ability to love others.

Then say:

Use the paper and pencils to make a short list of New Year's resolutions. These should be promises you intend to keep this year. After you have made your promises, exchange your list with a partner and talk about the choices you have made.

Close your devotion with a circle prayer or a time of silence.

#19: WHAT'S YOUR DREAM?

Themes: MARTIN LUTHER KING, JR., DAY, INCLUSIVENESS, COOPERATION

Scripture: Your young men will see visions,
and your old men will have dreams (Acts 2:17).

Preparation: a pair of binoculars, a microscope, a kaleidoscope, a pair of opera glasses

The Lesson

Gather the youth into a circle and pass around the various items. Ask the youth to take turns looking through the various lenses as they reflect upon the following question: How does each item help you to see your world differently?

After each person has looked through each lens, invite the teenagers to talk about their insights using the following questions:

• What new things did you see or think about as you looked through each lens?

• How does looking at something from a different angle or magnification reveal new insights?

• In what ways have we grown accustomed to looking at things in the same fashion?

• What new "lenses" might we need to see God's work in our world today?

Read aloud the beginning of Peter's Pentecost speech (Acts 2:14-21). Then ask:

What dreams and visions do you think Peter had for the world? What dreams and visions do you think Martin Luther King, Jr., had for America? How are these dreams being fulfilled today? In what ways are they unfulfilled?

Close by discussing what Martin Luther King, Jr., Day means for America and the church.

#20: CREATION POWER

Themes: MARTIN LUTHER KING, JR., DAY

Scripture: So God created humans to be like himself; he made men and women (Genesis 1:27).

Preparation: a Beanie Baby® or similar small, stuffed toy animal

The Devotion, the Object Lesson

Hold up a Beanie Baby® as you begin your talk.

Say:

One of the most recent toy crazes is for Beanie Babies®. These are small, stuffed toy animals that are discontinued or phased out of production after a time. However, no two Beanie Babies® are exactly the same—they are different colors, different styles, different textures, and even different prices. On the outside they look quite different, but on the inside, they are all the same.

The Creation story reminds us that God made human beings with as much variety as the plants, birds, and animals. Diversity and variety are built into the order of Creation. Just as there are many different varieties of flowers and trees, there are different varieties of animals and birds. Can you imagine how dull and boring the world would be if there were only one type of flower, only one type of animal?

Martin Luther King, Jr., Day is a reminder that God's variety and creation power extends to all people, too. We are different races, different sizes, different body types, and different sexes. But we are all children of God. We are all created in the image of God. Although we have different exteriors, on the inside we are the same. We bear God's image. Let's celebrate God's creative power by celebrating one another—in all our varieties and colors. When we learn to love one another, we are learning to love our Creator, too.

#21: SWEETHEART CAFETERIA

Themes: VALENTINE'S DAY, LOVE, FRIENDSHIP

Scripture: God is love (1 John 4:16).

Preparation: reservations at a fast-food restaurant, Valentine menus (see below)

The Meal

If you are looking for a creative meal or a perfect Valentine's Day outing for teenagers, try reserving an area or room at a local fast-food restaurant. Some restaurant's even have basements for this purpose. Before you arrive, however, prepare your own menu for the teenagers and give every item on the menu a "Valentine" theme. For example, here is a menu I have used several times for these Valentine dinners.

APPETIZERS
Engagement rings (onion rings)
Fig Leaves (salad)

ENTREES
The Casanova (chicken sandwich)
The Aphrodite (fish sandwich)
Cupid's Special (hamburger)
Hot Tub (chili)
Cupid's Arrows (French fries)

Love Potion (soft drink)

DESSERTS
Cold Shower (slush drink)
Cold Shoulder (ice cream)

(Note: Patrons should be advised that they are ordering all items at their own risk.)

#22: WHAT'S LOVE GOT TO DO WITH IT?

Themes: VALENTINE'S DAY, MARRIAGE, RELATIONSHIPS

Scripture: Be sincere in your love for others (Romans 12:9).

Preparation: a copy of a marriage certificate, a wedding ring, Bible, a married couple who is willing to talk about marriage

The Lesson

Form two groups (boys and girls) and invite someone to read aloud Colossians 3:18-19.

Ask:

What do these verses say about the nature of love and marriage?

After some discussion, invite the married couple to talk to the teens for ten to fifteen minutes about their marriage (joys, struggles, what marriage means to them, and so forth). Allow some time for teens to ask questions.

Pass around the copy of the marriage certificate and the wedding ring.

Ask:

Why do you think we call marriage "holy matrimony"? What do this piece of paper and the wedding ring represent? Why are promises important in marriage?

Ask the youth to ponder the following question as you read aloud 1 Corinthians 13: How would you describe the nature of love, as presented in this Bible passage?

Close by having both groups (girls and boys) offer their respective insights into what they have learned about love and marriage.

#23: THE LOVE BOWL

Themes: VALENTINE'S DAY, FUN

Scripture: Let love be your only debt! (Romans 13:8).

Preparation: plastic rings, a box, a tricycle, a gown, a tuxedo or men's suit, a stopwatch

The Game

Organize this game like a classic Olympic competition. Divide the group into teams of four (preferably two boys, two girls). Each person on the team will choose one event. Keep time with the stopwatch. Team with the shortest time wins.

1st Event—Get Me to the Prom on Time

The first person will ride the tricycle around a small track. Upon crossing the finish line he or she must tag the second person.

2nd Event—Prom Night (Two Players)

The second person must run from the track, put on the tuxedo or prom gown, then run and tag the third person, who must put on the remaining garment. Arm in arm they must dance around the track and tag the fourth and last person.

3rd Event—Ring Toss

The fourth person must attempt to toss rings into a small box at a distance of ten feet until he or she has successfully boxed five rings. Time is up when this person completes the ring toss.

#24: Letter to the President

Themes: PRESIDENTS' DAY, CITIZENSHIP, RESPONSIBILITY

Scripture: Obey the rulers who have authority over you (Romans 13:1).

Preparation: paper and pens

The Discussion Starter

Hand out paper and pencils and invite the youth to write a letter to the President of the United States. Allow ten to twelve minutes and then ask each teenager to read his or her letter (or divide the group into smaller groups if you have a large gathering).

Read aloud Romans 13:1-7. Follow with some questions for discussion:

- What do you think of the apostle Paul's belief that we should obey all civil authorities?
- What dangers, if any, do you see in this philosophy?
- Do you think that civil authorities, including U.S. presidents, are God's servants?
- How do we show respect for our leaders in a democracy?
- Have there ever been times in U.S. history when people should have disobeyed government officials or positions? When?
- How can we better support our government leaders today?

#25: NAME THAT PREZ!

Themes: PRESIDENTS' DAY, FUN

Scripture: All of you nations, come praise the LORD! (Psalm 117:1).

Preparation: none

The Game

If you are looking for some presidential questions to use in a trivia game or contest, here are some sticklers. (You may, of course, add some of your own.)

1. Which president had the shortest tenure in office? (William Henry Harrison)

2. Which president was known for his taste in fashion? (Chester A. Arthur "Dude")

3. Which president was known as the rough rider? (Theodore Roosevelt)

4. Which president had the longest tenure in office? (Franklin D. Roosevelt)

5. Which president was known as "Big Bill"? (William H. Taft)

6. Which presidents have "doctrines" named after them? (Harry S. Truman, James Monroe)

7. Which Presidents appear on Mount Rushmore? (Washington, Jefferson, Lincoln, T. Roosevelt)

8. Who was third president of the U.S.? (Thomas Jefferson)

9. Which president has the middle name "Quincy"? (John Quincy Adams)

10. Who was known as "Honest Abe"? (Abraham Lincoln)

11. Who was the youngest elected president ever? (John F. Kennedy)

12. Name the presidents who came before and after Jimmy Carter (Gerald Ford/Ronald Reagan)

CHAPTER TWO: SPRING

#26: A HANDFUL OF DUST

Themes: ASH WEDNESDAY, REPENTANCE, DEATH

Scripture: People who try to save their lives will lose them, and those who lose their lives will save them (Luke 17:33).

Preparation: a bowl of ashes or dust

The Devotion

Place a bowl of ashes or dust in the center of the group. As you give this talk, invite each person to reach his or her hand into the bowl and feel the ashes.

Say:

Perhaps you have been to a funeral or you have heard a pastor say, "Ashes to ashes, dust to dust." These words serve to remind us that we are all going to die someday and that our bodies will decay and return to the earth. Of course, no one likes to think about death, and we certainly don't want to think about our own death.

Today is Ash Wednesday—the day that begins the season of Lent, a period of forty days leading up to Easter Sunday. Traditionally Christians have used this day not only to remember that death is a part of life, but also to remember our need for God.

As you feel the ashes today, don't forget: We are nothing without God. God gives us breath, and life, and love. Without our Creator, we are nothing. Every day is a gift. We are who we are and what we are because of God's great mercy. We are dust. But we are also children of God. By turning to God, by asking for God's mercy, you and I can know the greatness of God's compassion for us.

Close the talk with a prayer or with the imposition of the ashes on the forehead or hand.

#27: GETTING IN FOCUS

Themes: ASH WEDNESDAY, REPENTANCE

Scripture: When God saw that the people had stopped doing evil things, he had pity and did not destroy them as he had planned (Jonah 3:10).

Preparation: a pair of strong prescription eyeglasses, an eye chart

The Devotion

Gather the group together and give everyone an opportunity to attempt to read the eye chart while wearing the pair of eyeglasses.

Then ask:

Why was it difficult or impossible to read the letters on the chart? ("It was too fuzzy," "Too blurry," "Not the right prescription.")

Say:

As we know, eyeglasses must provide the proper focus for us to see clearly. If the lenses are too strong or too weak, we will be unable to see things as they really are. The same can be true of life. Often we become self-absorbed or we focus on the wrong things, and we lose our perspective and our direction. Sometimes we focus only on the big things, but we cannot see all of the little things that need our attention.

Just as some of us need eyeglasses to see well, you and I need to keep our hearts and desires focused on the things of God if we are to live well. If we read an eye chart wrong, we say that we have made a mistake. But if we live wrong, that is what we call sin. Sin is anything that separates us from God or others.

Today, let's all put on some new spiritual glasses and turn again to God. If we do that, and truly mean it, God will help us see life in a new way. It is as if we are given new eyes. And we might even find that we have been missing out on many things that God wants to give us.

#28: ID CARD

Themes: LENT, FAITHFULNESS, DISCIPLESHIP

Scripture: There are different ways to serve the same Lord, and we can each do different things (1 Corinthians 12:5).

Preparation: instant camera, instant camera film, tape, felt-tip pens

The Affirmation

Here's an easy but effective affirmation that will have a positive effect on your group.

First, take a photograph of each teen and tape the photos to the wall (spaced three to five feet apart). After the photos have developed, give each person a felt-tip pen.

Say:

I'd like for you to create a Christian ID card for everyone in the group. To do this, you will need to write something positive on the bottom of each person's photo. This can be a positive trait you see in that person, or a talent that the person possesses, or an uplifting word or phrase. Keep your words brief and leave space for everyone to add a word or two.

Close with the Scripture reading and a circle prayer. Allow each person to take his or her ID card home.

#29: BANANA SPLIT

Themes: LENT, SPIRITUAL GIFTS, THE CHURCH

Scripture: The body of Christ has many different parts (1 Corinthians 12:12).

Preparation: ingredients for a banana split (ice cream, bananas, chocolate syrup, strawberries and other fruits, toppings, chopped nuts, whipped cream), large bowls, ice cream scoops, small bowls, serving and eating spoons

Friendship-Building

Divide your group into teams of two or three. Give each team the same amount of ice cream, toppings, and bananas. Have a fun contest to see who can build the most impressive banana split. Five to seven minutes should be plenty of time to complete a split.

Award prizes if you would like. Close by dividing the banana splits into smaller dishes for eating. While the youth are enjoying their dessert, read aloud the passage from 1 Corinthians 12:12-26.

Afterward, ask:

How is the church like a banana split? What did you learn about one another from working together?

#30: PENNIES FROM HEAVEN

Themes: LENT, PRAYER, SERVICE

Scripture: Finally a poor widow . . . put in two coins that were worth only a few pennies (Mark 12:42).

Preparation: none

The Service Project, Fundraiser

As a special Lenten offering for others, try challenging your congregation or youth to bring in their pennies during the first week of Lent. The second week of Lent, have them bring in nickels. The third week, ask them to bring in dimes. The fourth week, challenge them to bring in quarters. The fifth week, encourage them to bring in dollar bills. And the sixth week, have them bring in five dollar bills.

This fundraiser really works.

#31: A FAITHFUL FRIEND

Themes: LENT, FAITH, FRIENDSHIP

Scripture: We should honor God and try to be completely like him (2 Corinthians 7:1).

Preparation: two people willing to read or act out the parts

This brief skit may be used as part of a Lenten worship experience, or it could be used to lead into a discussion about faith or friendship. The parts may be learned or simply performed as a reader's theatre.

Skit (based on Luke 5:17-26)

A DISCIPLE: One thing I know—when you're with Jesus, wonderful things happen.

A FRIEND: When I heard that Jesus had come to town, I took a sick friend to see him. But there were so many people, and Jesus was inside a house.

DISCIPLE: I saw the sick man coming, being carried by his friends on a cot. There was no way that they could make it through the mass of people.

FRIEND: But I didn't give up. "Let's take our friend onto the roof," I said. "We can lower him down to Jesus."

DISCIPLE: They made a large hole in the roof and lowered their friend to Jesus.

FRIEND: "Rise up and walk," I heard Jesus say to my friend. "Your sins are forgiven."

DISCIPLE: Many people began to question Jesus. They wanted to know how he could forgive.

FRIEND: When my friend heard that he was forgiven, new life stirred within him. His feet and ankles grew strong and he stood!

DISCIPLE: Sometimes we need a friend. Sometimes we can make a difference to someone else.

FRIEND: Since that day, I've learned that I have to make an opening in my life for God. Sometimes, having faith takes a lot of work.

DISCIPLE: What about you? Are you a good friend? Do you need to make an opening in your life?

#32: ROOTS

Themes: LENT, DISCIPLESHIP

Scripture: They are like trees growing beside a stream (Psalm 1:3).

Preparation: a tree root, paper, pencils, posterboard, markers, Bibles

The Training Session

Pass out pencils and paper. Place the root in the middle of the group and ask the youth to list the important functions of a tree root. List as many as possible. Then say: As we can see, roots serve to nourish and strengthen a tree. Without roots there would be no support, no food, and no health. When a tree's roots get sick, the whole tree will die. You and I need roots, too. And that is what this training session is about.

Pass out Bibles and invite the group to read together Psalm 1:1-3. Ask: How are faithful people like trees? What happens when we are faithful?

Have a volunteer read Matthew 5:1-12 aloud. Using the posterboard and markers, number from 1-8 down the left margin. Reading the passage again verse by verse, ask the youth to list three insights for each "beatitude". Ask: How can we use these marks of discipleship to help our group? How can we apply these teachings to our youth meetings? What do you think would happen if we followed these teachings of Jesus?

Close by praying for each other by name. Make a summary of the session and send a copy to each participant.

#33: I AM THE CLAY

Themes: LENT, DISCIPLESHIP, SPIRITUAL GROWTH

Scripture: We are nothing but clay,
but you are the potter who molded us (Isaiah 64:8).

Preparation: modeling clay, Bibles

The Lesson

Give each teen a lump of modeling clay. Then ask the youth to fashion some type of earthenware jar, mug, or plate. Afterwards, choose one of the youth to read aloud Isaiah 45:9-11.

Invite the youth to divide into small groups to discuss these questions: How is fashioning clay like an act of creation? What do you think Isaiah was saying about the relationship between God and people? How is God like a potter? How are we like clay?

After discussion, ask the youth to destroy the clay items they have made and fashion new ones. Then choose another youth to read aloud Jeremiah 18:1-10 and Jeremiah 19:1-2, 10. In small groups, discuss these questions: How is Jeremiah's idea of God different from Isaiah's? Why would God want to start over with the clay? What does Jeremiah have to teach us about the nature of sin and repentance?

Give each teen a new lump of modeling clay. Close the lesson by reflecting on this question: How is forgiveness like starting over with a new lump of clay?

#34. THE HUMBLE OLYMPICS

Themes: LENT, HUMILITY

Scripture: Many who are now first will be last, and many who are last will be first (Matthew 19:30).

Preparation: assorted board games (chess, checkers, and Chinese checkers work best)

The Game

A sk the youth to define the word *humility*. Then read aloud Jesus' description of *humility* from Matthew 19:30.

Hand out the board games, with the following explanation:

When Jesus taught the disciples about the kingdom of God, he often turned everything upside-down. Jesus taught that the people in first place would be last, the people who were rich would become poor, and the lowliest people would be given the places of highest honor. But being humble is not easy. We actually have to work at it.

Today we are going to play some games. But the object of the games is not to win but to lose. In other words, whoever loses the game will record a win. And whoever wins the game will receive a loss.

Allow adequate time for each teen to play a game. Then ask:

How were you forced to think differently as you played this game? Why do you think it is difficult for us to allow someone else to win or to receive honor? What do you think Jesus meant when he said that the "first would be last and the last would be first in the kingdom of God"?

#35: THE PEBBLE

Themes: LENT, SIN, REPENTANCE

Scripture: If your right eye causes you to sin, poke it out and throw it
away (Matthew 5:29).

Preparation: small pebbles (one for each teen), Bible

The Devotion, The Game

As you begin, give each teenager a pebble and say:

Take off a shoe, place this pebble inside, and then put your shoe back on.

Next, lead the youth through a series of active calisthenics: running in
place, jumping-jacks, hopping, skipping, relays, and so forth. After five to
ten minutes, allow the teens to sit on the floor and remove their pebbles.

Ask:

How were you aware of the pebble while we were exercising? Why was it
difficult to think of anything else but the pebble?

Choose someone to read aloud Matthew 5:29-30. Then say:

What was Jesus saying about the nature of sin in this passage? How can a
little sin cause greater problems in life?

**Lead the group through another brief round of calisthenics. Again
sit on the floor and ask:**

How is removing a pebble from a shoe like removing sin from our lives?
How is God's forgiveness freeing? How is God's forgiveness helpful to us?

Close with prayers of confession or other prayers for one another.

#36: THE BIG PICTURE

Themes: LENT, FAITH, VISION

Scripture: Shout praises to the Lord!
He is good to us, and his love never fails (Psalm 107:1).

Preparation: a poster that has been cut into puzzle pieces

The Game

Before the meeting, purchase an inexpensive poster. Cut the poster into puzzle pieces and mix up the pieces. (You may glue the poster onto a piece of cardboard for greater firmness before cutting). If you have a large group, you may need more than one puzzle.

Allow the youth to work together to complete the puzzle. Afterward, ask these thought-provoking questions:

• What is the "big picture" in life?

• How can faith help us to put together the pieces of life?

• If there were an instruction manual for living, what would it be?

#37: FAMILY OF GOD

Themes: LENT, SERVICE

Scripture: All the Lord's followers often met together, and they shared everything they had (Acts 2:44).

Preparation: laundry baskets or large paper sacks

The Service Project, The Scavenger Hunt

Give each teenager a laundry basket or large paper sack at the end of a youth meeting. Ask group members to take the baskets or sacks home and fill them with various items and bring them back the following week. Award points for each item (and play in teams if you would like). Once the items have been collected, your group can take the goods to a food pantry or shelter, or you may distribute the goods directly to the needy.

Take-Home Scavenger Hunt

Canned foods (5 points each)

Boxed foods (10 points each)

Soap (5 points)

Laundry detergent (10 points)

Diapers (15 points)

Baby food (5 points per jar or box)

Socks (5 points)

Paperback books (5 points)

Peanut butter (15 points)

Brand-new clothing (15 points)

A new Bible (25 points)

Bottled juice (15 points)

Canned soup (10 points)

Blankets (15 points)

#38: Red Carpet

Themes: PALM SUNDAY, CELEBRATION

Scripture: "Blessed is the king who comes in the name of the Lord!" (Luke 19:38).

Preparation: a long, narrow strip of red carpet, Bibles

The Worship

Gather for worship by reading aloud Psalm 8. Then sing a favorite song.

Offer prayers on behalf of others, or invite the youth to offer brief prayers as a response to the following sentences:

God, we thank you for _____.

Lord, hear our prayers for _____.

Ask the youth to form two lines, facing each other. Place the red carpet in between the two lines; and, as one of the teens reads aloud Luke 19:28-44, have someone unroll the carpet. After the Scripture reading, ask for volunteers to offer brief reflections on what they heard.

Ask:

Why were the people praising God? What were they expecting Jesus to do or to be? What does it mean to "roll out the red carpet" for someone?

Follow this time of witness by repeating Luke 19:38 several times. See if some of the youth can repeat the verse from memory. Close with a song.

#39: WHO NEEDS A KING?

Themes: PALM SUNDAY, DISCIPLESHIP

Scripture: When Jesus came to Jerusalem, everyone in the city was excited and asked, "Who can this be?" (Matthew 21:10).

Preparation: a slick teen magazine full of pictures of teen idols

The Devotion

Read the account of Jesus' entry into Jerusalem from Matthew 21:1-11. Then say:

Palm Sunday was probably the most dangerous day of Jesus' life. When Jesus entered the city, many people were shouting, "Come save us! You are the new king and we welcome you into the city!" This activity was dangerous because, in the days of Jesus, there was only one person considered worthy of worship and praise: the Emperor of Rome. Anyone who made himself a king or was hailed as a king by others was quickly arrested and punished, usually by death. So Palm Sunday was not a relaxing day for Jesus.

Of course, there are many things that you and I can put in place of Jesus. We may have many kings and rulers. There may be many who receive our praise and adoration, including professional athletes, supermodels, the rich and famous, Hollywood celebrities. But there can be only one who is truly worthy of our worship: Jesus Christ.

On the day of palms, the people of Jerusalem were saying, "We want no king but Jesus. We will worship only him. He is the one we have been waiting for." You and I may not have an opportunity to welcome Jesus into our city, but we can welcome him into our hearts.

#40: THE BIG TABLE

Themes: HOLY THURSDAY, COMMUNION, THE CHURCH

Scripture: [Jesus] broke the bread and handed it to his apostles. Then he said, "This is my body, which is given for you" (Luke 22:19).

Preparation: bread, grape juice, a chalice (or cups)

The Sacrament

Try celebrating communion on Holy Thursday at a large table. Make sure that there are enough chairs for the youth group but also a few extra seats, which can be left vacant. If you are not able to serve communion, invite your pastor to preside at this event.

Open the time of communion by offering personal prayers or concerns. Then say:

Long ago, Jesus gathered at table with his disciples for a final Passover meal. At the end of the supper, Jesus took leftovers from the supper and gave them a special meaning. He told his followers that he was going away and gave them bread and wine as a memorial of his suffering and death. But Jesus also told his followers, "Where two or three are gathered together in my name, there I will be in the midst of them."

Tonight you and I have gathered for this memorial meal we call communion, or the Lord's Supper (Eucharist). But our table is large. In fact, there are extra chairs. Whenever we break the bread and share the cup, it is important to remember that God's table is bigger than any table we could ever arrange. During his ministry, Jesus made it clear that God's invitation was often rejected by the religious folks but accepted by those who were regarded as outsiders. God's table is a big table—large enough for all of us here and many more.

Ask:

Who could we invite to be a part of this table? Who can you see sitting in the empty chairs?

#41: REFRESHMENTS

Themes: HOLY THURSDAY, COMMUNION, JOY

Scripture: Then the disciples from Emmaus told what happened on the road and how they knew he was the Lord when he broke the bread (Luke 24:35).

Preparation: a cookie and small container of fruit juice

The Devotion, The Sacrament

Before communion, give this brief devotion:

There is a funny story about a little girl who came to church one day. When she noticed the cups and bread on the altar, she said, "Oh, look, Mommy! Refreshments!"

Perhaps you remember when you enjoyed having a refreshment after school (and some of you still might). Maybe you ate a cookie and milk or drank a little juice to give you that afternoon pick-me-up. Some of you might even come home from school and drink a cola or eat potato chips. You may not call it a refreshment, but you're getting something out of those extra calories that your body craves or needs.

We may not consider communion a refreshment, but receiving the bread and cup can certainly be refreshing. This moment reminds us that our spirits need to be refreshed from time to time. We need strength. We need forgiveness. And we need to remember that God cares for us. Actually, we may not think that there is much power in a small piece of bread and a sip of juice; but when Jesus is present, powerful things happen. And that kind of love can be the most refreshing thing in the world.

#42: CROSS WORDS

Themes: GOOD FRIDAY, SALVATION, FORGIVENESS

Scripture: After Jesus drank the wine, he said, "Everything is done!" He bowed his head and died (John 19:30).

Preparation: Bibles, paper, markers

The Lesson

Divide the group into seven teams. Assign one of the Bible passages to each team: Matthew 27:45-46; Luke 23:34; Luke 23:39-43; Luke 23:44-46; John 19:25-27; John 19:28-29; John 19:30. Ask each team to read their Bible passage and reflect on two questions:

• How do you think Jesus was feeling when he said these words from the cross?

• How do these words make you feel when you hear Jesus say them?

After each team has reflected on its individual passages, read aloud and in succession the seven passages from the cross. Hand out paper and pencils. Ask the teenagers to do one of two activities as a reflection on the cross:

1. Draw a picture of a contemporary situation or place where people are suffering.

2. Make a list of ways people suffer today.

Close by asking:

How does the cross (Jesus' suffering) address the suffering in our world today? What are some of the root causes of people's suffering? How does Jesus' death on a cross give you hope?

#43: SILENCE!

Themes: GOOD FRIDAY; PRAYER

Scripture: At noon the sky turned dark and stayed that way until three o'clock (Matthew 27:45).

Preparation: Bibles, a collection of devotional books for teens, a list of prayer concerns, markerboard, markers

The Prayer

If you want to give your teenagers some silent time, Good Friday provides a wonderful opportunity. Since we live in a world of high activity, constant sound, and saturation of images, try to provide a space where your youth can feel a sense of solitude and quiet even if they are near others. Your youth room may not be the best place. Perhaps you could go to a park or slip into another room in your church.

Hand out Bibles and ask the youth to read about the suffering and death of Jesus. Write these two passages on the markerboard: Mark 15; John 19. Also provide (at your discretion) a collection of devotional guides, a prayer list, or other materials that will help the group focus and reflect for at least thirty minutes.

Close in silence or, if you would like, ask the youth to talk about what they learned from the Bible or from their devotional reading.

#44: WITNESS

Themes: EASTER, RESURRECTION, EVANGELISM

Scripture: Jesus isn't here! He has been raised from death (Luke 24:6).

Preparation: a female reader (based upon Mary Magdalene) to read the following monologue

The Monologue, The Drama

If I were to tell you about the extraordinary events that have taken place recently, I doubt that you would believe me. Sometimes I can scarcely believe it myself! My friend was Jesus, a man who had been a healer and a great teacher. But many of us also regard him as the Messiah, the one whom God sent to redeem the world from sin and death.

I and many other friends had come to Jerusalem with Jesus a few days ago. But the crowds turned against him, demanding that he be crucified. Jesus was taken to the leaders of the people and handed over to the Romans to be whipped and tortured. I watched as he was killed on a cross. But even there, he asked God to forgive those who had put him to death. Even as he was dying his heart was pure and his love flowed into my life.

I watched as Jesus' body was taken from the cross and placed quickly into a rock tomb. The Sabbath was approaching and there was no time to anoint his body with burial spices. All hope had fled from us, and we went back to our homes to rest on the Sabbath.

On the first day of the week, however, I came to the tomb with the spices, accompanied by the other women. When we arrived at the tomb, we found that the giant rock had been rolled away. There was no one inside. The body of Jesus was no where to be found. Suddenly a young man said to us, "Are you looking for Jesus of Nazareth, who was crucified? He is not here. He is risen from the dead."

Trembling with fear, I ran from the tomb and told the other disciples what I had seen and heard. But they did not believe me. Now I come to tell you— Jesus is alive! That is my witness. Do you believe me? Can you believe that Jesus lives?

#45: GRAVE DANGER

Themes: EASTER, RESURRECTION, HOPE

Scripture: When the disciples saw the Lord, they became very happy (John 20:20).

Preparation: Bible, photocopies of the litany below

The Worship

Years ago, Christians would gather in cemeteries to celebrate Easter. Where better to anticipate resurrection than in a graveyard? If you have an opportunity to visit a cemetery at Easter, use this brief worship service to heighten the joy of the day.

Gather in song or silence, and circle around several tomb stones. (This will be especially powerful if you can locate markers of friends or relatives in the group.) Invite the youth to read aloud the names on several tombstones. Pause in silence. And then ask the youth to offer names of relatives and friends who have died.

Read aloud the resurrection appearance found in Luke 24:36-53. Ask the youth to offer words of praise and thanksgiving for the hope of resurrection. As a time of witness, ask the youth to offer expressions of faith, reflecting on the following question: Why do you believe that Jesus is alive?

Join together in this brief litany as a closing:

Leader: Today is a day of celebration.

Youth: Christ is risen!

Leader: We serve a God of the living, and not of the dead.

Youth: Christ is risen, indeed.

Leader: Even though we die, yet shall we live.

Youth: Because Jesus lives, nothing can separate us from the love of God.

#46: WATER WORLD

Themes: **EASTER, BAPTISM**

Scripture: We were baptized, so that we would live a new life, as Christ was raised to life by the glory of God the Father (Romans 6:4).

Preparation: a bowl of water

The Sacrament, The Lesson

Say:

Did you know that in the early church, most converts to the faith were baptized on Easter Sunday? After a period of training, known as catechism, new converts were dressed in white and were welcomed into the church as redeemed individuals. The gift of water and the belief that water represented renewal, rebirth, and new life, became the identifying mark of Christianity. Let's hear how the apostle Paul talks about baptism:

Read aloud Romans 6:1-11; then pass around the bowl of water, asking each youth to dip his or her hand into the water.

Ask:

Why do you think water is such a powerful reminder of our need for God and of God's love? Why is water associated with cleansing and birth?

After discussion, pass the bowl around the circle again. Invite those who wish to participate to remember their baptisms. This may be done by the pastor, or youth may take turns applying the water to one another's forehead with the words: "Remember your baptism, and be thankful." (Note: Should you have questions about the nature of baptism or its significance, check with your pastor.)

#47: RISE UP!

Themes: EASTER, JOY

Scripture: Christ will rule until he puts all his enemies under his power, and the last enemy he destroys will be death (1 Corinthians 15:25-26).

Preparation: a parachute

The Game

Gather in an open, grassy area with the parachute. Space the youth evenly around the edges of the chute and practice raising the chute several times before playing this game. Once the youth have mastered working together to achieve a good draft under the chute, play the game this way:

This is a game that requires quick reflexes and cooperation. Have the youth place the parachute on the ground and have the youth sit, evenly spaced around it. One person will get up and begin walking clockwise around the chute. When this person taps another teenager on the head, that teen must simultaneously stand and yell, "Rise Up!" With that command, everyone else also stands and raises the chute as high as possible before pulling it down. The teen who was walking tries to run under the parachute before the others can pull the chute to the ground. If the walker succeeds, he or she continues to walk and tap people until he or she is caught under the chute. Continue play until everyone has had an opportunity to be the walker.

#48: COCOONS AND BUTTERFLIES

Themes: EASTER, RESURRECTION, NEW LIFE

Scripture: But God loved us so much that he made us alive with Christ (Ephesians 2:5).

Preparation: four boundary cones, several adult helpers

Friendship-Building Game

This tag-style game requires two teams and a wide outdoor space. One team is called "Cocoons," and the other team is called "Butterflies." The game has no boundaries (unless, of course, you want to make some).

To begin, place the Cocoons inside the four boundary cones. (This area can be as large or small as you like, but it should have enough space for everyone on the team to move about freely.) The Cocoons may not leave this area unless they are tagged by a Butterfly. The Butterflies, of course, are free to roam the rest of the playing area—after all, they're butterflies!

The goal of the game is for the Butterflies to tag every Cocoon player without going inside the coned area. Cocoons may move around and reach over the line but may not cross the boundary until after they have been tagged. At that point they become Butterflies, too.

This would be easily achieved, of course, if not for the Keepers (adult helpers who guard the Cocoons and try to keep the Butterflies away). If a Keeper tags a Butterfly, the Butterfly becomes a Cocoon and must go inside the coned area.

Play continues until all of the teens are the same—either a Butterfly or a Cocoon. This is a high energy game and one that kids will enjoy. (Note: If you don't have an adequate number of adult helpers, you may use a sufficient number of youth as Keepers.)

#49: FAITH AND DOUBT

Themes: EASTER, FAITH, DOUBT

Scripture: They saw him and worshiped him, but some of them doubted (Matthew 28:17).

Preparation: Bibles, paper, pencils, marker\board, markers

The Lesson

Handout Bibles and write the following Scripture references on the chalkboard: Matthew 28:17; Mark 16:11-14; Luke 24:10-11; Luke 24:40-41; John 20:24-29. Ask the youth to read these passages (or in small groups) and respond to the following question: What do each of these Resurrection stories have in common? (Answer: the disciples doubted.)

Ask:

Why, do you think, did each of the gospels make such a strong case for doubt and faith? Why is it difficult to believe that someone could rise from the dead?

Say:

The fact that the gospels record doubt in equal parts to faith is a great testimony to the mystery of the Resurrection. In fact, most of us are people who have doubt and faith mixed within us. We want to believe, but something (maybe common sense) holds us back. Or we want to doubt, but something compels us to accept what we cannot explain. The apostle Paul even says that the gospel message itself and the Resurrection of Jesus is a mystery (1 Corinthians 15:51; Ephesians 6:19). And how does one go about explaining a mystery? The good news is that Jesus never talked about having lots of faith. Rather, he talked about having faith as a grain of mustard seed (Matthew 17:20). You see, God can use even a little faith, even if most of our lives are composed of doubt.

Give each teenager a paper and pencil and ask him or her to write down why he or she believes in the Resurrection of Jesus (or why he or she doubts it). Close with a prayer asking God to aid us in our unbelief.

#50: EASTER PEOPLE

Themes: EASTER, THE CHURCH, FRIENDSHIP

Scripture: Christ Jesus chose you to be his very own people
(1 Corinthians 1:2).

Preparation: eggs, pins, bowls, dyes, markers

Friendship-Building

Give each youth an egg, or divide the group into teams of two. Encourage the youth to experiment with hollowing out an egg for decorating—an ancient art that is fun and rewarding. To hollow out an egg, punch a pin hole in each end of the egg, lean over a sink or bowl, and blow the yolk and egg whites out. This takes a few minutes and some care; but once the shell is hollowed, it can be rinsed with water and dried.

Follow this procedure with dying (or markers). The egg shell may also be scratched or carved with the pins to create intricate designs and patterns. Allow at least an hour for this activity, and work together to create some beautiful works of art.

Follow the egg decorating by reading aloud 1 Corinthians 15:35-58 to the group.

#51: GREEN THUMB

Themes: ST. PATRICK'S DAY, FUN

Scripture: Let all things praise the name of the LORD (Psalm 148:5).

Preparation: washable green paint

The Game

St. Patrick's day may be an Irish festival, or a patron day; but for most folks, it's a day to dress in green. And if you want to go totally green with your youth group, try mixing up a little green tempera paint and see how far your kids will take this unique variety of tag. Be sure to play this game outdoors and don't be afraid of the mess.

Begin by choosing one or two people to be "green thumbs." These teens must dip their hands into green paint and try to tag other people. Anyone who gets greened also becomes a "green thumb." Continue until everyone has been marked with green prints.

For variety, you may also establish "bases," areas where players will be safe from the "green thumbs." Or, if you want to go totally green, fix up the first "green thumb" to look like Frankenstein's monster—green from head to foot—guaranteed to make a few people run for their lives.

#52: APRIL FOOL

Themes: APRIL FOOL'S DAY; TRUTH

Scripture: Only a fool would say, "There is no God!" (Psalm 14:1).

Preparation: Write up a few of your own April Fool's stories (stories that aren't true).

The Game

Challenge your group's GQ (gullibility quotient) by mixing in the following *true* stories with a few April Fool's stories of your own creation. See if the group can spot the truth among the foolishness. Sometimes fact is stranger than fiction.

1. In 1995 a man walked into a bank and demanded money. The bank teller, sensing that the robber was one brick shy of a full load, told him, "I'll be glad to give you the money if you'll sign for it. It's a bank policy. All robbers must sign for the money." The fellow gladly complied, signing not only his name but also his address to the form. Police picked him up at the same address a few hours later.

2. President George Bush, in a 1992 interview, commented that he did not like broccoli. The story was worldwide news. A major broccoli producer shipped 10 tons of broccoli to the White House in protest. *Women's Day* magazine sponsored a recipe contest on "How to Get the President to Eat Broccoli." Due to all of the publicity, broccoli sales rose 40 percent.

3. In March 1995, an inmate escaped from a community release center in South Carolina. He was captured when he went back and tried to claim a paycheck.

4. Michael Jackson once said in an interview that his favorite song was "My Favorite Things," sung by Julie Andrews in *The Sound of Music*.

5. When Fidel Castro led his first revolutionary attack on a military post in Cuba, he forgot his glasses and could barely drive a car, much less aim a gun.

#53: WISE UP!

Themes: APRIL FOOL'S DAY, WISDOM

Scripture: Only a fool rejects wisdom and good advice (Proverbs 1:7).

Preparation: several "advice columns" from newspapers

The Discussion Starter

Gather the youth into a circle and read aloud several questions submitted to advice columnists. (These questions should be relatively easy to obtain from your local paper.) However, instead of reading the columnist's answer, allow the youth to offer their own insights to other people's problems. Then read aloud the columnist's answer and see how the youth respond to it.

Divide the group into teams of four or five, and give each team one of the following topics: dating, family, school, work, or sports. Ask each team to write two questions about their topic, which could be sent into an advice columnist. Exchange these questions between the groups and see what kind of advice youth give to youth.

Then ask:

Why is good advice difficult to offer? Why do you think so many people read advice columns? What biblical or spiritual insights do you think are important to remember?

Themes: EARTH DAY, STEWARDSHIP, CREATION

Scripture: The LORD God put the man in the Garden of Eden to take care of it and to look after it (Genesis 2:15).

Preparation: various plants, trees, flowers

The Service Project

Check with your church trustees to see if you can arrange for the youth to make your church grounds more beautiful and tidy. The youth could meet at the church on Earth Day to plant flowers or perhaps a tree and to clean up the yard. Many trustees might also grant you a small stipend to purchase plants.

Additionally, the youth could check with city officials about cleaning up road sides, planting flowers in public parks, or beautifying an area. You might also be able to organize a church Earth Day, sponsored by the youth, as an encouragement for other church members to participate in the projects or to learn more about pollution and what it means to be good stewards of God's creation.

#55: THE TAX MAN COMETH!

Themes: TAX DAY, STEWARDSHIP, FAITHFULNESS

Scripture: Then Jesus told them, "Give the Emperor what belongs to him and give God what belongs to God" (Mark 12:17).

Preparation: Bibles, blank tax forms, pencils

The Lesson

Give each youth a tax form and ask each of them to write in his or her name, social security number, and other pertinent information at the top. Ask them also to declare any income or taxes paid.

Then say:

April 15 is a day that many Americans fear. It is the day when they must declare to the Internal Revenue Service how much money they made, what they are worth, or how much they owe in taxes. Many people hate this day so much that they wait until the last day to send in their forms.

Ask:

Why do we place so much value on our money? Why do you think information about money and income is often guarded more fiercely than information about sex, family secrets, or even one's privacy? Why do you think most people dread the thought of paying taxes?

Hand out the Bibles and ask the youth to read Mark 12:13-17. Ask the youth to talk with partners about this passage and what it might mean for us today.

Ask:

What parallels do you see between the teaching of Jesus and people's attitudes about money and taxation today?

End the lesson by asking the youth to talk about the following issues as an entire group: How much should we give to God's work? How much should we give to government? What does it mean to be a good steward of one's financial resources? How much does God expect us to give?

#56: SHADOWS

Themes: GROUNDHOG DAY, FUN, CREATION

Scripture: God said, "I command lights to appear in the sky and to separate day from night and to show the time for seasons, special days, and years (Genesis 1:14).

Preparation: a bright spotlight or slide projector

Friendship-Building Game

Before the youth meeting, fix the spotlight so that when you turn it on, it will cast shadows onto a vacant wall (a slide projector will work equally well). When the youth arrive, invite them to sit on the floor in front of the light source.

Also, before the meeting, prepare small slips of paper, each containing the name of an animal, object, or active verb. (Examples: kangaroo, guitar, or running).

Give each teen a slip of paper, which they are not to show to anyone else. Offer these instructions:

Every spring there is a tradition that groundhogs determine whether we will have a long or short winter. If the groundhog sees its shadow and goes back into its hole, we have more bad weather coming. If the groundhog doesn't see its shadow, that means spring and good weather are just around the corner. Today let's have some fun with shadows—making them, that is. Each of you will be given an opportunity to use your hands to create the object or the action on your slips of paper.

Play the game individually just for fun; or if you like, you may divide the group into teams, give each person two minutes, and award points for each correct guess.

#57: MAMA MIA!

Themes: MOTHER'S DAY, LOVE, FAMILY

Scripture: Children must always obey their parents. This pleases the Lord (Colossians 3:20).

Preparation: blank business cards or heavy paper cut into 2-by-3 cards, markers

The Affirmation

I have discovered that Mother's Day (and Father's Day) is often a painful time for teenagers—particularly for those whose parents are divorced or separated. Because of this pain, I have generally shied away from talking about mothers and fathers and, instead, chosen to focus on the Christian family or the family of God. However, if you know your group's composure and heart, you might use this Mother's Day affirmation.

Hand out the blank business cards and the markers. Say:

Honoring our parents is more than just a feeling. To honor someone is also to act. Toward that end, I would like for each of you to prepare an "action" card that you can give to your mother. This card should contain a promise from you to your mother, which you intend to keep. Examples might be "I promise to clean my room this week," "I will cook a meal tomorrow night," or "I'm going to wash the car and watch my brother so that you and Dad can have a nice evening together."

Allow a few minutes for the youth to complete their promise cards. Close with prayer or a reading from James 5:10-11.

#58: SWEET ROSES

Themes: MOTHER'S DAY, LOVE, FAMILY

Scripture: Our love for each other proves that we have gone from death to life (1 John 3:14).

Preparation: Hershey's Chocolate Kisses®, green chenille stems (or craft stems), red cellophane, clear glue

Fundraiser

These sweet roses, in addition to being a great fundraiser, will also provide a tasty treat when folks are ready to eat them. To make the sweet roses, stack two unwrapped Hershey's Kisses® together at their bottoms, wrap tightly in red cellophane, and glue. Attach a green chenille stem (with leaves if you prefer) to the cellophane top to create a sweet rose. Sell the roses individually or by the dozen. If you would like, you may also use yellow and pink cellophane to create other varieties of roses.

#59: R.I.P.

Themes: MEMORIAL DAY, LOYALTY, HONOR

Scripture: The LORD blesses each nation that worships only him (Psalm 33:12).

Preparation: an American flag

The Discussion Starter

ivide the youth into small groups, and unfurl an American flag in one corner of the room. Ask the youth to talk about their impressions of America and what their country means to them.

Afterward, ask these questions to get your youth talking:

• What do you like about America?

• What do you dislike?

• If you could change one thing about your country, what would it be?

• Would you ever be inclined to give your life for your country? Why or why not?

• Rank, in order of allegiance, what is most important in your life? (family, God, friends, self, truth, an so forth).

If you have people in your congregation who have lost a loved one in a military conflict or a war, such as World War II, the Korean War, the Vietnam War, or the Persian Gulf War, invite them to talk to your group about the meaning of Memorial Day.

#60: FIRE!

Themes: PENTECOST, THE HOLY SPIRIT, POWER

Scripture: He will baptize you with the Holy Spirit and with fire (Luke 3:16).

Preparation: candle, matches, Bibles, markerboard or large sheets of paper, markers

The Lesson

Place the candle in the middle of the group and light the wick. Go around the circle and ask the teenagers to offer one word that would describe fire. Write these words on a whiteboard or a large sheet of paper.

Then say:

There are many aspects of fire: heat, light, purification, power, destruction, danger, radiation. Fire was also seen as a mysterious power and was used to offer burnt offerings to God. Later, flame was used as a symbol of the Holy Spirit. Why do you think this was so?

Divide the youth into groups of three or four. Hand out Bibles. Invite the youth to read Luke 3:3-17 and discuss the following questions in their groups:

- What did John the Baptizer teach about the relationship between Jesus and the Holy Spirit?

- What did John say about the nature of Jesus' baptism and ministry?

- How does the notion of fire (as we talked about earlier) apply to John's image of the Holy Spirit?

As a closing prayer, read aloud Hezekiah's prayer, as found in Isaiah 38:10-20.

#61: GOD'S BREATH

Themes: PENTECOST, THE HOLY SPIRIT

Scripture: Then he breathed on them and said, "Receive the Holy Spirit" (John 20:22).

Preparation: a windsock

The Devotion

Hold up the windsock as you begin the following talk:

Have you ever been to a small airport and seen a windsock blowing in the breeze? A windsock is rarely used in larger airports—we have superior technology now—but is still used by pilots of smaller craft to tell them which way the wind is blowing, how strongly, and how steadily. As you might imagine, the wind is vitally important when one is flying an airplane. Sudden wind shifts or strong gusts can make a difference to a pilot.

When Jesus appeared to the disciples (according to the Gospel of John), he breathed on them and said, "Receive the Holy Spirit." Jesus had made clear to his followers that the Holy Spirit would guide them, empower them, and comfort them in the days ahead. Like a windsock, the Holy Spirit can tell us which way God is leading, how strong God's leading is, and which way we should go. Sometimes knowing God's will takes much prayer and study. Sensing God's direction involves talking to others and listening to their spiritual advice.

As you think about the Holy Spirit's power and direction in your life, what important factors would you include in knowing the will of God?

#62: SPIRIT PEOPLE

Themes: PENTECOST, THE HOLY SPIRIT

Scripture: On the day of Pentecost all the Lord's followers were together in one place (Acts 2:1).

Preparation: Bible, paper, pencils

Friendship-Building

Read aloud the Pentecost account from Acts 2. Emphasize that the first Christians were together in one place and shared all things. They worked together and provided for one another's needs.

Divide the group into two teams and give each team a piece of paper and a pencil. Provide the following instructions:

Consider the following questions: If Christianity were condemned by the government and the church was suddenly forced to go underground, what would you consider to be the important aspects of a life together? What items would be necessary to sustain a community of faith in such a harsh environment?

Segregate the two teams so that neither will be able to hear what the other is saying. Allow fifteen to twenty minutes for group discussion. Bring the two teams together and invite them to talk about their ideas.

Ask:

How do you see the church living out the spirit of Acts 2 today? What can we do better to make everyone feel part of the church?

#63: SAY YES!

Themes: CONFIRMATION, FAITH, THE CHURCH

Scripture: The church of the living God is the strong foundation of truth (1 Timothy 3:15).

Preparation: photocopies of the affirmation below

Affirmation

Celebrating confirmation and other decisions of faith among our teenagers can be both meaningful and unifying. This affirmation can be used in a youth group setting to affirm the faith of those who have recently been confirmed or recognized in the church. This affirmation is based upon 1 Timothy 3:16 and 2 Timothy 1:9-10.

Leader: Christ was preached to the nations.

Youth: People in this world put their trust in him.

Confirmands: We believe Jesus came to show the kindness of God.

Leader: Jesus Christ came as a human and was taken up in glory.

Youth: Christ our Lord defeated death.

Confirmands: And brought us the good news.

Leader: The good news of Jesus Christ shines like a light.

Confirmands: And offers us life that never ends.

Leader: I am the church.

Youth: You are the church.

Confirmands: We are the church together.

All: God saved us and chose us to be a holy people.

#64: MEMORIES

Themes: GRADUATION, FRIENDSHIP

Scripture: A true friend is closer than your own family (Proverbs 18:24).

Preparation: a collection of photographs, and memorabilia for your graduating seniors, blank videotapes, video camera

Friendship-Building

Perhaps one of the saddest and most celebrated occasions in any youth group is when seniors graduate from high school. Plan ahead to make this moment special for your graduates by asking the other youth members to assemble a collection of memorabilia for them. This collection can consist of photographs (taken on retreats, at camps, and on mission trips), videos, and special mementos from the high school years. Most of the high school youth will likely have photos and other items they can contribute to the collection.

Once you have amassed the memorabilia, make a video of the items and send a copy of the tape to each of your graduates. You may also slip in parting shots and poignant stories told by the other youth members. And don't forget to put in a few words of your own.

#65: LOVE LINES

Themes: GRADUATION, INTEGRITY, LOVE

Scripture: Love should be your guide (1 Corinthians 14:1).

Preparation: paper, pencils, newspaper personal ads (romance connection)

Friendship-Building

Hand out the newspaper personal ads, the section featuring romance ads. Allow the youth to read a few of these. Hand out the paper and pencils.

Say:

Many people are looking for romance and companionship in our society, as these small ads attest. Perhaps people are lonely, or maybe they are trying to meet someone who will fulfill a fantasy or meet a deep personal need. Regardless of the reason, the Scriptures tell us that love should be our aim in all things, in all relationships, and that we should have a personal integrity in the way we deal with others.

Ask each youth to write a personal ad for the romance section of the newspaper.

Say:

This ad should reflect something about who you are, what you value, and the type of person you hope to meet.

(Sample: SWM, age 17, loves horses and movies, wants to meet SWF, age 17, to share quiet evenings and television and youth meetings.)

Once the teenagers have written their ads, ask the seniors to read their personal ads first. Invite the other youth to offer insights about the seniors, what they appreciate about them, what they will miss, and what they believe they will find in the way of love and joy in the future. Close with a prayer for all the seniors, and ask the other teens to give each senior a hug.

#66: YEARBOOK

Themes: GRADUATION, FRIENDSHIP

Scripture: Keep being concerned about each other as the Lord's followers should (Hebrews 13:1).

Preparation: purchase a copy of your local high school yearbook or yearbooks

Friendship-Building

Another great way to celebrate graduation with your seniors is to buy a high school yearbook. (Be sure to purchase a yearbook from each of the high schools that your seniors attend.) Have everyone in your youth group sign the book and make it available to the seniors before they graduate. Invite the other teenagers to write a word of praise, remembrance, or best wishes for each of the graduating seniors on a separate sheet of paper. This sheet could be photocopied and sent along as a graduation gift.

In addition, you could use the yearbook as a kind of youth group archive. Keep these yearbooks in a file; and before long, you will have amassed a nice history of the youth group. Be sure to pass this tradition along if you ever move. Better yet, find a person in your church who would take this on as a ministry each year. Your seniors will love this.

CHAPTER 3: SUMMER

#67: SCHOOL'S OUT!

Themes: SUMMER VACATION, JOY

Scripture: Keep your Creator in mind while you are young! (Ecclesiastes 12:1).

Preparation: none

Peer Counseling

One of the most beneficial summer events our youth group organized was a peer mentoring service for the summer months. We set aside a four-week period of time in which older teenagers (juniors and seniors) would be available to mentor younger teens in a variety of activities. Some teens volunteered to help younger teens develop their athletic skills in such sports as tennis, basketball, and soccer. Other teens concentrated on academic pursuits and volunteered to tutor younger teens in subjects such as algebra, chemistry, and English.

The results of this summer program really helped the younger teens, but the older youth were admired by many of their peers and learned that they could use their gifts effectively. Parents also appreciated the opportunity. Most teens volunteered an hour or two a week, so the load wasn't heavy; and the activity also encouraged new friendships and support within the group.

#68. REST HOME

Themes: SUMMER VACATION, REST, PEACE

Scripture: You are better off to have a friend than to be all alone (Ecclesiastes 4:9).

Preparation: none

Group-Builder

Youth ministry during the summer months can be difficult. Many teenagers work, play in sports leagues, or are absent due to family vacations and other commitments. Even though the summer months can be a down time for your group, don't let that discourage you from offering support and encouragement to your teenagers.

One way to get around the problem of smaller groups in the summer is to provide an "open house" area for youth to drop by, chat, and enjoy a refreshment. One group I know has a Friday night time, offering youth an opportunity to gather informally, play games, and eat snacks. Naturally, you will want to organize this time around your schedule or the availability of other adult volunteers. Although summer is a busy time for most teens, for others it is the prime season for breaking the law and mischief. Take advantage of this time by offering a safe alternative for kids who just want to "hang out" and relax.

#69: GROWING PAINS

Themes: SUMMER VACATION, GROWTH, FAITH

Scripture: Everything on earth has its own time and its own season (Ecclesiastes 3:1).

Preparation: a yardstick, pencil, Bibles, index cards

The Lesson

At the beginning of the summer vacation, measure each teenager in your group by having them to stand with their back against a wall. Use a yardstick to measure from the floor and make a hash mark on the wall with a pencil. Label each mark with the teenager's name.

At the end of the summer vacation, gather the group together again and see how much each person has grown (you will be amazed at how much taller many of the boys will be). Gather the group into a circle, hand out Bibles, and ask everyone to read Ecclesiastes 9:11-16 and 10:1-20.

Then ask:

What type of growth is the wise teacher talking about in these passages? Do you agree with the teacher (9:16) that wisdom is more important than physical strength? What other insights did you receive from reading the wisdom of the teacher?

Hand out the index cards and pencils. Ask each teenager to write down a favorite verse from this portion of Ecclesiastes and use it as a bookmark when school begins. Close with a prayer for one another, and allow the youth to express any concerns they may have about a new school year.

#70: TOUGH CHOICES

Themes: CHURCH CAMP, FELLOWSHIP, FRIENDSHIP

Scripture: My dear friends, stand firm and don't be shaken. Always keep busy working for the Lord (1 Corinthians 15:58).

Preparation: none

Friendship-Building

This is a wonderful get-acquainted activity that you can use with youth around the evening campfire. If you have a large group, you may want to divide into small groups or, better yet, ask each teen to choose a partner. Switch partners after every question to keep the activity moving along.

Allow your teens to get acquainted and begin to provoke talk by asking a series of crazy questions. Most are funny, but some are thought-provoking or challenging. Emphasize that each teen should give a response to the question and tell the partner why he or she made a particular choice.

1. Would you rather do fifty push-ups or fifty sit-ups?
2. Would you rather go to the dentist for a drilling or to the doctor for a shot?
3. Would you rather know how to play the guitar or the violin?
4. Would you rather make straight *A*'s in school or be captain of the high school team?
5. Would you rather be injured in a car wreck or be the cause of someone else's injury?
6. Would you rather eat lima beans or spinach?
7. Would you rather die in a bungee jumping accident or get struck by lightning?
8. Would you rather have a friend or be a friend?
9. Would you rather give a gift or receive a gift?
10. Would you rather swim in applesauce or tartar sauce?

#71: WANTED!

Themes: CHURCH CAMP, FORGIVENESS, LOVE

Scripture: Let the Spirit change your way of thinking and make you into a new person (Ephesians 4:23-24).

Preparation: old "wanted posters" from the post office or police station, Bibles

The Lesson

If you are looking for a camp lesson on forgiveness, bring in a few "wanted posters" of various criminals (your post office or local police should be able to supply you with copies). Pass these out to the youth, break the youth into teams, and ask the teams to discuss the following questions:

• What background or mistakes do you think led this person to a life of crime?

• What might have helped this person make better choices in life?

While they are still in groups, have the teens discuss the following questions:

• Have you ever broken the law? If so, how?

• What are some mistakes or bad judgments you have made that could have led to something worse?

• Who helped you get back on track?

Hand out Bibles. Invite the youth to read Matthew 5:43-48.

Then ask:

In what ways is Jesus' teaching a radical change from the way we live? Do you think that it is possible to forgive those who have wronged us? Why or why not? Who might be considered your enemy today?

End the lesson in small group prayer. Pray first for the people on the wanted posters. Invite the youth to pray for one another also and to offer words of forgiveness and encouragement where needed.

#72: ON THE MOVE

Themes: CHURCH CAMP, OUTREACH

Scripture: Moses used to set up a tent far from camp. He called it the "meeting tent" (Exodus 33:7).

Preparation: old bed sheets (king size, if possible), markers, Bibles, dowels (7 foot length), hammers

The Project

Divide the youth into teams of four or five. Give each team a bed sheet, markers, four dowels, and a hammer. Gather the teams into a circle and read aloud Exodus 25:8; 26:1-30.

Say:

Obviously we don't have all of the materials to build a "meeting tent" as described in Exodus, but we can try to build a replica. You may also use the markers to decorate your tent with symbols and other decorations that you believe were described in Exodus.

After each group has completed a tent, gather the teams together for this reflection:

When the people of Israel were wandering in the wilderness, they were a mobile people. They were always on the move. They had to be ready to go to where the food and water was. Later, God asked the Jewish people to be a light to all the nations of earth. Their outreach and witness was for the world.

Likewise, Jesus stressed to his disciples, "Go into all the world and proclaim the good news!" As Christians, we have always been a mobile people, ready to be on the move so that we could meet the needs of others.

Ask:

How do you see this activity of the church in your community? How do you see the church reaching out to serve others?

#73: HOLY PLACES

Themes: CHURCH CAMP, WORSHIP, GRACE

Scripture: Then Jacob became frightened and said, "This is a fearsome place! It must be the house of God and the ladder to heaven" (Genesis 28:17).

Preparation: a large cross, shovel, a colorful drape for the cross

The Worship

Church camp usually offers many possibilities for worship sites. Often, traditions catch hold in a camp, and certain places take on a sacred space or feel. Some teenagers may also have special places in mind for worship. If your teens have expressed an interest in a certain location, allow them to make the place sacred by erecting a large cross in the ground. Give them a colorful drape for the cross as well, and invite them to lead a worship service in that setting.

As a possible worship idea, see if there are teens who would like to sing special music or play an instrument to begin the service. Other teens could offer prayers, Scripture readings, and drama.

For Scripture lessons about sacred places, why not read one or more of the following passages: Genesis 28:10-22 (Jacob consecrates Bethel); 1 Kings 5:1-6, 13-17 (Solomon builds the Temple); Matthew 26:17-19 (Jesus eats with the disciples); Matthew 28:16-20 (the risen Jesus meets the disciples on a favorite mountain).

#74: STARS AND STRIPES

Themes: FOURTH OF JULY, SYMBOLISM

Scripture: Put on all the armor that God gives (Ephesians 6:11).

Preparation: an encyclopedia (containing the history of the American flag), Bibles

The Lesson

Before the youth meeting, assign a teenager to write a brief report on the history and symbolism of the American flag. Offer the encyclopedia as one source.

Open the meeting by allowing the teenager to read his or her report to the group.

Ask:

Why do we need symbols such as a flag? What other symbols are important to you?

Say:

Jesus used many symbols and metaphors in his teachings. A metaphor is an image that is used to compare one thing with another. For example, Jesus said, "You are the salt of the earth." He said, "You are the light of the world." The ideas of salt and light are not literal but symbolic of a deeper spiritual reality.

Divide the group into smaller teams, and ask the teens to read Ephesians 6:11-17.

Then ask:

What symbols are used in this passage to talk about the Christian life? If this passage were to be presented in modern-day terminology or symbols, what might we use? How are symbols helpful or harmful in understanding the spiritual dimensions of our faith?

If time allows, ask the youth to draw other symbols of the Christian faith or take a scavenger hunt in the church, looking for symbols and other graphic expressions of faith.

#75: INTO THE FUTURE

Themes: **FOURTH OF JULY, VISION**

Scripture: I saw a new heaven and a new earth (Revelation 21:1).

Preparation: *Star Trek* video, or a *Star Wars* video, VCR, TV, Bible

The Lesson

Prepare to show a favorite clip from a *Star Trek* or *Star Wars* video*. Before you show the clip, however, ask the youth to ponder this question:

• What similarities and differences do you see between the future presented in this movie and contemporary society?

After the youth have watched the scene, allow them to offer their insights. Once everyone in the group has expressed an opinion, have a volunteer read aloud Revelation 21:1-7. Ask the youth to ponder the following question:

• What similarities and differences did you hear between the future presented in this Bible passage and contemporary society?

Following this discussion, remind the youth:

This is the Fourth of July, the day in which the Declaration of Independence was signed. Such a step involved bold foresight and courage. Vision and boldness about the future was also required.

Ask:

What kind of future do you think our ancestors envisioned for us? What is the vision you have for the future? How do God and faith fit into the picture?

---

* Under the law, for-profit and nonprofit organizations are required to have a public performance license to show movies, which include purchased and rental videocassettes.

Home vidoecassettes may be shown, without a license, in the home to "a normal circle of family and its social acquaintances" (Section 110.1 of the Copyright Act) because such showings are not public. All other showings of home videocassettes are illegal unless they have been authorized by license. Even "performances in 'semipublic' places such as clubs, lodges, factories, summer camps, and schools are 'public performances' subject to copyright control" (Senate Report No. 94-473, page 60; House Report No. 94-1476, page 64).

To obtain a license or if you have questions about your need for one, contact Harald Bauer, Executive Vice President of The Motion Picture Licensing Corporation, at 800-515-8855 (fax 203-270-8830).

Licensing information is from "The Fine Print," *Reel to Real,* © Abingdon Press.

#76: VACATION CHALLENGE

Themes: SUMMER VACATION, DECISIONS, FRIENDSHIP

Scripture: Such a large crowd of witnesses is all around us! (Hebrews 12:1).

Preparation: a scavenger hunt instruction sheet

The Game

Before you lose many of your youth to family summer vacations, why not give them a little something to do while on the vacation? It's easy. Prepare a scavenger hunt list for youth to use on their family outings. See who can amass the most points from their summer outings. Better yet, your group is sure to collect some unique items.

Example List

A postcard showing the hotel where you lodged (5 points)

Your passport (5 points)

A photo of you and your family taken on your vacation (10 points)

Beach sand (5 points)

Map of city where you stayed (10 points)

Travel books (5 points)

Leftover suntan lotion (5 points)

Airline meal (25 points)

Photo with hunk or gorgeous chick taken on your vacation (15 points)

Restaurant menu (20 points)

#77: ABBA!

Themes: FATHER'S DAY, LOVE, FAMILY

Scripture: Jesus said, "My Father has never stopped working, and that is why I keep on working (John 5:17).

Preparation: Bibles, index cards, pencils

The Lesson

Keep in mind that Father's Day, like Mother's Day, can be a source of pain for many teenagers. Not everyone has pleasant attitudes or memories of his or her father. If you know your group well, however, you should be able to gauge the helpfulness of this lesson.

Ask the youth to sit in a circle. Give each teen an index card and a pencil. Invite each teen to write down two questions he or she has about God. Collect these cards and hold them until later. While still in a circle, invite each teenager to tell a brief story or observation about his or her father. These could be funny stories, things the teens appreciate about their fathers, or memories.

After each teen has talked, hand out Bibles and invite the teens to read John 10:7-18.

Ask:

What image does Jesus use to talk about himself and his Father (God)? What does Jesus say about his Father in this story? How would you describe the Father whom Jesus is describing in this passage?

Following discussion, shuffle the index cards and hand them out to the group. Allow each teenager to choose one of the two questions listed on his or her card and read it to the group. Use the remaining time to address the questions the teens have written about God.

#78: THE BIG NUMBER FIVE

Themes: FATHER'S DAY, RESPECT, LOVE

Scripture: Respect your father and your mother (Exodus 20:12).

Preparation: Bibles

The Discussion Starter

A sk the youth to read Exodus 20:1-17 (with special emphasis on the fifth commandment: respect your father and mother). Follow the reading with these thought-provoking questions:

• Why do you think this commandment appears fifth among the Ten Commandments?

• What does it mean to respect your father and mother?

• This is the first commandment with a promise: what promise does it give?

• How might this commandment be the foundation upon which the subsequent commandments rest?

• Do parents always command our respect? Why or why not?

#79: ROAD SIGNS

Themes: DRIVER'S EDUCATION, RESPONSIBILITY, RULES

Scripture: It makes good sense to obey the Law of God (Proverbs 28:7).

Preparation: paper, markers

The Game

Divide the group into teams of four or five. Give each team five sheets of paper and markers. Explain the game. Here's how to play.

Everyone who learns how to drive must also learn the rules of the road and the signs that direct the flow of traffic. However, I'm sure that we'd all like to add a few road signs of our own. Here's your opportunity. Create five new road signs that you would like to see along the roadside soon. These signs can be funny or serious, and they should also have a unique shape to help drivers identify them.

After each team has created their five signs, have the youth do some role playing, if you would like, holding the signs up to see if unsuspecting motorists would be able to follow the directions.

This game can be a lot of fun. Some of the more creative signs I've seen include a Road Kill sign, a Mud Slide sign, a 155 Mile Per Hour sign, and a Honking Zone sign.

#80: THE TICKET

Themes: DRIVER'S EDUCATION, FORGIVENESS, RESPONSIBILITY

Scripture: A truly good friend will openly correct you (Proverbs 27:5).

Preparation: a traffic ticket

The Devotion

Begin the devotion by asking if any of the participants have ever received a traffic ticket. Hold up the ticket as you start your talk:

Receiving a ticket from a police officer can be a very nerve-wracking experience. Some people feel embarrassed when they receive a ticket. Others feel angry. Still others feel stupid or ashamed. Regardless of how we feel, however, a traffic ticket is a reminder that we have broken a law (even though, many times, we don't want to admit that we have).

But remember, a ticket is not an indictment of our character. A ticket does not prohibit us from being a good friend, taking responsibility, or even coming to church. It is simply a reminder to us that we share the road with many people and that we need to be more careful and watch out for one another. Receiving a ticket might make us feel many things, but we can always start over again.

That's a bit like what our faith tells us about forgiveness and responsibility. You and I are trying to live well, to follow the teachings of Jesus. But we often fail. Our failure, however, does not mean that we cannot continue to be a disciple. No matter what we feel, God's forgiveness and love is available to us.

#81: DO YOU KNOW THIS TEEN?

Themes: BIRTHDAY, COMMUNITY, CELEBRATION

Scripture: Kind words are like honey—
they cheer you up and make you feel strong (Proverbs 16:24).

Preparation: photograph of the teenager who is celebrating a birthday

Affirmation

If your group enjoys playing tricks on people and preparing surprises, they will love this birthday idea. First, get a photograph of the teen who is celebrating a birthday (but don't let him or her know that you have the photo). Be sure that you choose a person who is not easily offended. Make an enlarged photocopy of this photo and add your own embellishments—such as mustache, sideburns, freckles, scars—with a felt-tip marker. Or if you have a scanner, computer, and a graphics application, you can distort the photo so that it looks like the reflection in a fun-house mirror.

Next, prepare written copy above and beneath the photocopy. For example, you could make a wanted poster, a Do You Know This Teen? poster, or a Dangerous Criminal poster. Create your own funny or poignant copy about the birthday person, make additional copies, and tack them up on the youth room wall. If you want to take this joke further, create a yard sign that can be placed outside the person's house or bedroom.

#82: THE PRIZE

Themes: BIRTHDAY, MYSTERY, GRACE

Scripture: God blesses everyone who has wisdom and common sense (Proverbs 3:13).

Preparation: a box of kid's cereal

The Devotion

Purchase a box of kid's cereal that advertises a prize inside. Allow one of the teens to open the box of cereal and look for the prize as you begin the devotion.

Say:

Some cereal companies have sold their product by advertising that a prize is inside the box. These simple prizes appeal to the desires of children (and maybe even teenagers) who don't necessarily enjoy the cereal but certainly want what's inside the box. It seems that the more mysterious the prize inside the box, the more children want to see what's inside.

Having a birthday is a bit like discovering a hidden prize. When we look back on another year in our lives, we can often see the blessings we have missed, the opportunities we had, and the ways in which we have grown. A birthday is meant to remind us that God has been good to us. God gave us life. We belong to God. The very fact that we were born is a kind of mystery in itself, and God's grace is the greatest prize of all.

This year on your birthday, you will likely open many gifts. Like a box of cereal, you will not know what's inside. But you can recognize that God's gift to you is another year of life, good friends, and people who care about you. These are the kinds of gifts that never grow old.

#83: FOR YOUR EARS ONLY

Themes: BIRTHDAY, FRIENDSHIP

Scripture: Just as iron sharpens iron,
friends sharpen the minds of each other (Proverbs 27:17).

Preparation: audiocassette recorder, blank audiotape

Friendship-Building

As a surprise gift for the birthday person in your group, invite the other members of your group to record their birthday greetings and best wishes. The youth could also include favorite jokes, memories, or songs.

Box up the tape and send it in the mail or think of a creative way to deliver the tape on the person's birthday—perhaps as some type of a singing telegram.

#84: THIS IS YOUR LIFE

Themes: BIRTHDAY, FAMILY, LIFE

Scripture: Live in harmony by showing love for each other (Philippians 2:2).

Preparation: a surprise gathering of friends and relatives for the birthday person

Affirmation

Every now and then you might want to organize a surprise birthday event for one of your youth. With some extra planning and energy, you could arrange for friends and relatives to do a miniature version of *This Is Your Life*, a vintage television show that used friends and famous personalities to surprise the guest of honor. You could also arrange to do a version of the classic "roast," where friends and family provide humorous observations about the guest of honor.

Either way, be sure that the birthday person does not know about the event, and make certain that the party stays upbeat and positive in nature. As an extra touch, you could also incorporate favorite songs and readings into the event.

#85: CAKE WARRIORS

Themes: BIRTHDAY, COOPERATION

Scripture: A friendly smile makes you happy,
and good news makes you feel strong (Proverbs 15:30).

Preparation: cake mixes and various icings and decorations

Friendship-Building

This is a messy birthday event, but one that can provide a rich reward of sweetness when completed. You will need access to the church kitchen, or an oven and cooking utensils if you are doing this in a house.

Divide the group into teams of three or four. Give each team a cake mix, icing, and other decorations. Challenge the teams to see who can make the best birthday cake for the guest of honor. Naturally, if your time is limited, you could have the cakes already baked and allow the youth to do the decorating.

Don't forget to include plenty of food colorings for the icing. You may also provide party favors, balloons, and candles if you wish. Close the time together by reading the Scripture verse and praying together.

#86: TEACHERS

Themes: FIRST DAY OF SCHOOL, LEARNING, WISDOM

Scripture: Let instruction and knowledge mean more to you than silver or the finest gold (Proverbs 8:10).

Preparation: none

The Devotion

Begin the devotion by asking two questions and allowing the youth to respond:

• Who are some of your favorite teachers?

• Why or how have these teachers influenced you?

Say:

It is amazing to realize how much time each of us spends in the presence of teachers. We have about 6 hours of classroom time each day, 5 days a week, for 42 weeks a year. That's over 1,200 hours of classroom time each year. Multiply that by 12 years and you've had more than 14,400 hours of teachers by the time your graduate from high school. It is no wonder that teachers are some of the most influential people in our lives.

But have you ever stopped to thank a teacher for what he or she provides for you in the way of inspiration and learning? Going back to school each year may seem like an easy thing to most teenagers; but for teachers, it requires a lot of work to get things set up, to prepare lesson plans, and to grade papers. Did you know that you can inspire your teachers by offering words of praise and thanks? You can help encourage them by being an example at school—having patience, being obedient, speaking well of others. These are the things that Jesus taught. So, as you go back to school this year, think about the people who make it possible. You are blessed. There are many people who care about you; and as the Scripture in Proverbs 8:10 states: "Let knowledge mean more to you than silver or gold."

#87: APPEARANCES

Themes: FIRST DAY OF SCHOOL, PRIDE, INTEGRITY

Scripture: Wicked people bluff their way,
but God's people think before they take a step (Proverbs 21:29).

Preparation: none

The Discussion Starter

If you have an opportunity to meet with your teenagers before the first day of school, use this brief discussion starter to get your youth thinking about their discipleship.

Begin by reading the Scripture verse aloud, then ask:

What kinds of attitudes and appearances do you expect to encounter on the first day of school? Do you think that it is easy or difficult to be yourself on the first day of school? What challenges are most apparent on the first day of school? How do you see God helping you to meet the challenges of a new school year?

Close by asking the youth to express any fears or concerns they may have about the school. Gather into a circle and pray for one another. And, if you would like, give each of the teenagers a small gift to help them remember your concern for them.

CHAPTER FOUR: FALL

#88: OUT OF WORK

Themes: LABOR DAY, SPIRITUAL GIFTS, CARE

Scripture: The Spirit has given each one of us a special way of serving others (1 Corinthians 12:7).

Preparation: newspaper "jobs available" ads, Bibles, nametags, markers

The Lesson

As the teenagers arrive, hand out tags and markers. Ask each person to make a nametag.

Say:

Write your name on the tag, and underneath your name, write an occupation or job you hope to do some day. This can be a job you dream about, or a work that you are actually considering pursuing after high school.

After each person has completed a nametag, ask the youth to sit on the floor. Give each teenager a section of newspaper "job available" ads (hint: Sunday papers are best). Ask the teenagers to circle those jobs that look appealing to them.

Once the youth have completed their search, ask each person to find a partner and talk about the following questions:

• Which jobs looked appealing to you? Why?

• How did your job search match up with your dream job on your nametag?

• What skills or special abilities would be required to do the jobs you circled?

Following discussion, hand out Bibles and ask the youth to read along from 1 Corinthians 12:1-11. Ask the youth to talk with their partners about the special gifts and abilities they would bring to their job.

Close with a celebration of work and the opportunities God gives us to help others.

#89: ALL WORKED UP

Themes: LABOR DAY, HELPFULNESS, WORK

Scripture: Hard work is worthwhile,
but empty talk will make you poor (Proverbs 14:23).

Preparation: envelopes, index cards with different careers written on them

The Game, The Drama

This creative game involves no preparation on the part of the "actors," but it can nevertheless provide a glimpse into the difficulties of talking about work. Before the meeting, prepare several index cards—each card containing the name of a different occupation. (Hint: The more off-beat the occupation, the funnier this game is. For example, occupations such as "belly dancer," "politician," and "electrical engineer" would be sure hits.) Place each card in an envelope.

Explain the game this way:

Each of you will be given an index card containing the name of an occupation. Each of you will then get a turn to talk about this occupation but without using the name or any derivative of the occupation itself. For example, if your occupation is "doctor," you cannot say, "I doctor people."

Allow each teen to attempt an explanation. Some will be quick. Others may take some time. If you wish to make the game more difficult, play this game as charades, not allowing the kids to talk at all. In this instance, they would communicate only through gestures. You could also play this game using teams.

#90: DISCOVERIES

Themes: COLUMBUS DAY, GUIDANCE, ENCOURAGEMENT

Scripture: The LORD will always guide you (Isaiah 58:11).

Preparation: outdoor challenge area or access to hiking trail, blindfolds, Bible

Training Session

Some of the best training events take place when the exertion is physical as well as mental. Arrange to take your leadership team to a state park or an outdoor area where you can use a hiking trail. (Note: Be sure that the trail is free of major impediments such as large tree roots and rocks or drop-offs.)

Divide the group into two teams. Give each team a trail map and a blindfold and ask them to choose one person to "lead" the group along the trail. Stress to the teams that the person who is blindfolded must "lead" the group (but do not define what *lead* means). Set a return time, and allow the groups to journey the trail.

When the teams return, gather as one group and ask:

How did the blindfolded person lead your group? How would you describe the type of leadership you experienced?

Following discussion, point out that Columbus Day is a celebration of the discovery of America by Europeans. Say:

When we think about Columbus sailing the ocean, we think of someone who was blazing a new trail, going where no one had gone before—at least, not up until then. But leadership is not always about being the one to blaze the trail for others. In Christian tradition, a leader can be someone who demonstrates the qualities of strength, encouragement, or vision. Leaders are humble.

Read aloud 1 Timothy 3:1-13. Ask:

What did you hear about leadership in this passage? If you were to do this trail again, how might the blindfolded person lead the group (other than being the first one down the trail)? How can we best serve as leaders in our group?

Express joys and concerns and close with a prayer or with a reading from Isaiah 58:6-14.

#91: THE LANGUAGE OF GOD

Themes: WORLD COMMUNION SUNDAY, WORSHIP, THE CHURCH

Scripture: God wants everyone to be saved and to know the whole truth (1 Timothy 2:4).

Preparation: a tape of people speaking in other languages (a language-learning tape), audiocassette players, Bibles, communion elements

Worship, Sacrament

As the group gathers for worship, begin playing tapes of people speaking in other languages. Allow the teenagers to listen to these various languages for a few minutes without explanation.

Then say:

Today is World Communion Sunday—a day when Christians all over the world come together at the Lord's Table. We do not speak the same languages, wear the same style of clothing, eat the same foods, or share the same culture and art. Yet we are one people in Christ.

Sing one or two songs, then read aloud John 15. Ask the youth to reflect upon this passage and offer words of insight or testimony.

Invite the pastor or celebrant to lead the group in the Lord's Prayer and offer communion. Close with silent prayer or with the sounds of the languages.

If time allows, ask one or more of these questions for discussion:

What makes the notion of a world communion special or meaningful to you? How is the Holy Spirit involved in uniting the church?

#92: CASTING LOTS

Themes: VOTING DAY, CHOICES, LEADERSHIP

Scripture: They drew names, and Matthias was chosen to join the group of the eleven apostles (Acts 1:26).

Preparation: a voting ballot

The Devotion

Hold up the voting ballot as you retell this story of the election of Matthias:

Did you know that voting has been a part of the church since the beginning? After Judas Iscariot hanged himself, the apostles were left with a "vacancy" among the twelve. Before the Pentecost celebration in Jerusalem, they gathered together in the same room where they had eaten the last supper with Jesus. They said, "Hey, let's take a vote! Any suggestions?" The other apostles agreed that someone should be elected, but it had to be a person who had been with the movement from the beginning of Jesus' baptism until the end. They talked among themselves and finally settled upon two candidates.

That day there were two nominees for the twelfth apostle. One man was Joseph Barsabbas, whom everyone called Justus. The other person was Matthias. After praying, the disciples cast lots to see who would be chosen. Matthias was elected.

While this method of voting may seem strange to us today, it was most effective. Perhaps they threw dice to determine a winner, or maybe they drew straws. Some people believe that casting lots was like drawing names from a hat. But regardless of how it was done, there was an election. We continue to follow this tradition in our political and social arena by electing representatives from among the people.

Ask:

What qualifications do you think a social or political leader should have today?

#93: SWORDS AND SHOVELS

Themes: VETERANS DAY, WAR, PEACE

Scripture: They will pound their swords and their spears into rakes and shovels (Isaiah 2:4).

Preparation: a sword and a shovel

The Discussion Starter

Gather the group around the sword and the shovel. Read aloud Isaiah 2:2-5.

Ask:

- What is the vision of the prophet Isaiah in this passage?

- Why do you think people have always longed for peace, for the absence of bloodshed?

- Why do you think Americans have often talked about fighting "the war to end all wars"?

- According to Isaiah, how will true peace be accomplished?

- How do you think true peace can be accomplished in our time?

Say:

If you would like to make the discussion more powerful, convene the group at a local veterans' memorial or other marker. Chances are, there is a monument of some type in your hometown.

#94: FACING OUR FEARS

Themes: ALL SAINTS DAY, HALLOWEEN, ASSURANCE

Scripture: A real love for others will chase those worries away (1 John 4:18).

Preparation: scary masks, large sheets of paper (or overhead projector), markers

The Devotion

Ask one or more of the teenagers to wear the scary masks. Then invite the group to talk about the greatest fears they have in life. Write these fears on the large sheets of paper (projector).
Then say:

Most people associate Halloween with fear—fear of death, fear of dying, fear of evil. But when we come to know the true power and trustworthiness of God, many of the fears we have in life melt away. Fear, however, is a natural and good feeling. Without fear we would make many stupid mistakes, hurting ourselves and others in the process. Without fear, we would not have enough wisdom to flee when true dangers present themselves.

One of the ways people deal with their fears is by making fun of the fear itself. That, in fact, is part of the origin of Halloween, which means "all hallows eve." People were naturally afraid of death and dying, and so they decided to face their greatest fear by poking fun at death. In 1 John, we are told that perfected love casts out fear. That is to say, when we become certain of God's love, we don't have to be afraid anymore. It's as if God is the parent who comes in at night and tucks us in, turns on the night light, and tells us that there are no monsters. In God's great love, all fear melts away.

We can remove our fears by serving others. When we abandon our lives in service, we often discover that our fears lessen as our friendship and love deepens. As you and I think about our fears now, I hope that we will see that just as God has protected and redeemed those who have come before us, God will protect and redeem us, too. Even from death itself!

#95: SPIRITUAL ANCESTORS

Themes: ALL SAINTS DAY, HALLOWEEN, THE CHURCH

Scripture: Every one . . . died. But they still had faith, even though they had not received what they had been promised (Hebrews 11:13).

Preparation: list of those who have died in the past year from your church, Bibles, markerboard, markers

The Lesson

Hand out Bibles and invite the youth to read Hebrews 11:1-20; 32-40. Afterward, write on a chalkboard the names *Abraham, Sarah, Rahab,* and *Other Ancestors*. Ask the youth to describe the ways in which each of these people lived by faith, how they were faithful, or in what ways they could be considered examples to us today.

Gather the youth into a circle and say:

In the early church, people who had died in the faith were regarded as being part of the great "heavenly host" who praised God forever and ever. In many respects, saints were those who were not only believed to be examples of the faith, but also those who could intercede on our behalf before God. You and I know many saints, too. They may not be people who are mentioned in the Bible, but they are people who have influenced us and have been a part of the church we know.

Slowly read the names of those who have died in the past year. After the reading, ask the youth to comment on the people they knew. Ask the youth to tell why a particular individual had an impact on their life.

To close, read aloud Revelation 7:9-17. Ask:

What does this vision tell us about the nature of God's people? What does this vision tell us about what God desires for us? In what ways do you feel connected to those who have died in the faith?

#96: BRAVE HEARTS

Themes: ALL SAINTS DAY, HALLOWEEN, FUN

Scripture: Keep on being brave! (Hebrews 10:35).

Preparation: photocopies of the list below

Discussion Starter

Many people associate Halloween with evil, darkness, and fear. However, we can also use this time to talk about our fears, to tame some of the feelings we have about death and darkness, and to realize the strength God provides.

Here is one way to engage your group in a discussion of our fears and faith. This activity may be done in small groups if need be. The first list of questions below can be used as a discussion starter or may be presented at the beginning of a Halloween party. To deepen the discussion, share responses to the second set of questions as a time leading into prayer or a devotion.

Part 1: The Fears

The most frightening experience of my life was when _____.

The worst day of my life was when _____.

My greatest fear in life is _____.

Part 2: The Faith

I feel brave when I think about _____.

The greatest fear God has helped me overcome is _____.

My greatest triumph in life has been _____.

#97: THANKSLIVING

Themes: THANKSGIVING, SERVICE

Scripture: Do your best to improve your faith (2 Peter 1:5).

Preparation: a sign-up sheet for various services that the youth will perform for others

Service Project

As Thanksgiving approaches, begin to talk to your youth about the meaning of service to others and what it means to "live thankfully." Ask the youth to begin to think about "Thanksliving" instead of "Thanksgiving."

Make a sign-up sheet for the youth to indicate ways they would be willing to help someone else over the holiday season. Examples might include shovel snow, clean house, sit with a child, or drive someone to the store.

Once you have a list of youth who are willing to put their faith into action, advertise the various opportunities to the congregation. Allow others to sign-up for a youth helper or to elicit the help of a youth by advertising phone numbers.

You'll not only be helping others, but your group will also gain a positive spirit and visibility within the congregation.

#98: GIVE THANKS

Themes: THANKSGIVING, PRAISE

Scripture: Praise the Lord of lords.
God's love never fails (Psalm 136:3).

Preparation: Bibles, grocery sacks

Discussion Starter

For a quick worship time before Thanksgiving, offer this moment of reflection for the youth. Give each person an empty grocery sack.

Ask:

- Why do you think Thanksgiving is a holiday centered around the significance of food?

- In what ways is food harmful as well as helpful to us?

- How do you think your life would be different if you were able to eat only one meal per day?

- If you could fill your grocery sack with words of thanks, what would you place inside?

#99: PLUCK!

Themes: THANKSGIVING, FUN

Scripture: Everyone who serves the LORD, come and offer praises (Psalm 134:1).

Preparation: large turkey feather or ostrich feather, masking tape

The Game

This is a highly active game that requires both skill and speed (on the part of the "turkey") and cooperation (on the part of the "pluckers").

Explain the game this way:

To begin the game, one person will be chosen as the turkey. The turkey will be given a large feather, which will be taped to the seat of his or her pants. The turkey may run anywhere he or she chooses (within the boundaries) and will be pursued by the pluckers, who are trying to pull the feather from the turkey. The pluckers, however, must cooperate with each other to get the feather, as each plucker has a partner and the two are taped together at the ankles.

Choose the turkey, set boundaries, and make sure that each plucker has a partner. Partners should be taped together at the ankles with masking tape. When the turkey gets "plucked," choose a new turkey and begin again.

#100: THE MAGIC WORDS

Themes: **THANKSGIVING**

Scripture: With all my heart I praise you, Lord (Psalm 138:1).

Preparation: child's bib

The Devotion

Hold up the bib to begin the devotion. Say:

The earliest manners parents try to teach their children probably involves the use of the words *please* and *thank you*. Many parents try to instill these manners into their children at meal times, insisting that if a child asks for a drink of juice, the child say, "Please." Or when a child receives the drink, he or she must say, "Thank you." These two words have often been referred to as "the magic words." They are words that make things happen, that make other people feel good.

Thanksgiving is a time to use these same magic words in our relationship with God. This national holiday is a reminder that every one of us needs to pause to say "please" to God—for God is willing to offer us very much. Likewise, we have the human need to say "thank you." God has given us food, clothing, shelter, and an abundance of goodness that is life itself.

Being thankful is far more than simply observing a holiday, however. For the Christian, thanksgiving should be an everyday attitude. Our demeanor and lifestyle can be a celebration of the goodness of God. We may no longer wear bibs when we eat, but we have not outgrown the need to say "please" and "thank you" to God—the giver of all good things. Thanks be to God!

Close with a reading from Psalm 138, and ask the youth to express their thanks in prayer.